PRAISE FOR *KEE*

Before reading *Keeping the W...* ... ...y social studies classroom for what it was: brick walls, desks, and a few colorful posters. Today, I see magic seeping through the cracks of every space. *Keeping the Wonder* reignited my passion for student engagement and learning with every turn of the page.

—Dr. Jacob Bauer Zebley, high school social studies teacher and 2015 Cecil County Teacher of the Year

From personal stories, practical advice, and research-based strategies, *Keeping the Wonder* is a book you will reach for time and again. After reading, you'll start looking not just at your own classroom and curriculum through the lens of wonder, but the world around you. A must read for any teacher who is looking to bring that sense of curiosity and love of learning back into their classroom.

—Caitlin Mitchell and Jessica Cannata, cofounders of EB Academics and bestselling authors of *The Empowered ELA Teacher*

Abby, Ashley, Jenna, and Staci have written the book that all educators have been waiting for: inspiration to (re)invigorate their classroom instruction while providing rigor, depth, and synthesis with their approach to specific lessons. From the awesome workshops they have conducted for years, drawing educators from around the nation in droves, these amazing educators have proven they are rock stars. Reimagining how we teach and engage our students is a priority, and *Keeping the Wonder* gives practitioners permission to create wonder, curiosity, and, yes, fun, in the classroom!

—Dr. Angelyne Collins, library media specialist, Brookwood High School, 2021 Gwinnett Media Specialist of the Year, and 2020 Georgia Library Media Association Exemplary Media Program

If there ever were "perfect timing," it might be *right now* for this practical yet truly inspirational book! Whether you are beginning a career in teaching, or just returning after long periods of "virtual" practice, this book has a spark for everyone. From ideas for catchy repurposed furniture to provide an engaging atmosphere to instructional strategies grounded in research-based practices, consider "the wonder" of this new book! Become a Wonder Maker and bring curiosity, surprise, freedom, and inspiration to your teaching practice!

—Nate Ridgway and Dr. Angelia Ridgway, coauthors,
Don't Ditch that Tech: Differentiation in a Digital World

KEEPING THE WONDER

KEEPING the WONDER

AN EDUCATOR'S GUIDE TO MAGICAL, ENGAGING, AND JOYFUL LEARNING

By Jenna Copper, Ashley Bible, Abby Gross, and Staci Lamb

Keeping the Wonder: An Educator's Guide to Magical, Engaging, and Joyful Learning
© 2021 Jenna Copper, Ashley Bible, Abby Gross, and Staci Lamb

All rights reserved. No part of this publication may be reproduced in any form or by any electronic or mechanical means, including information storage and retrieval systems, without permission in writing by the publisher, except by a reviewer who may quote brief passages in a review. For information regarding permission, contact the publisher at books@daveburgessconsulting.com.

This book is available at special discounts when purchased in quantity for educational purposes or for use as premiums, promotions, or fundraisers. For inquiries and details, contact the publisher at books@daveburgessconsulting.com.

Published by Dave Burgess Consulting, Inc.
San Diego, CA
DaveBurgessConsulting.com

Library of Congress Control Number: 2021939152
Paperback ISBN: 978-1-951600-87-7
Ebook ISBN: 978-1-951600-88-4

Cover and interior illustrations by Sienna Youngsun Kim
Cover and interior design by Liz Schreiter
Editing and production by Reading List Editorial: readinglisteditorial.com

FOR OUR KTW COMMUNITY:
DEDICATED TO YOUR ENERGY AND
PASSION FOR EDUCATION

CONTENTS

INTRODUCTION

*Jenna

When this book was in its early stages, I started taking notes. No, not the kind of notes you would expect from an English teacher. Instead, this was more of a fluid stream of consciousness, a sticky note shoved in my clutch, an autocorrected observation jotted in my Notes app, a fifteen-second video lost to the abyss that is my cell phone video library—you get the picture.

I didn't tell anyone at first because I wasn't sure how to explain it. After all, I wasn't even sure what I was collecting in the first place. All I can say is it felt right.

I was collecting *something*. It sure wasn't fancy data. Rather, it was a *feeling*. It was a smile, a head tilt to the side to express "hmm?" An epiphany.

It was *wonder*.

If, as you're reading this, you're wondering to yourself, "What in the world is she talking about?" then you're beginning to experience what I'm talking about. Hang with me; I promise it will be worth it.

Let me backtrack a bit. I have two children, ages eight and five, three years apart almost to the day. And I love watching them interact with the world around them. That's why my observations were so imprecise: I was trying to analyze my experience while I was living it. Over time, I started to notice something: my children seem to have a sixth sense, and that sense is wonder.

As it turns out, many psychologists argue that we do not have a sixth sense, but rather a multitude of little-known senses. Taste, sight, touch, smell, and hearing are only the beginning. In fact, some researchers, like Bruce Durie writing for *New Scientist*, believe we have as many as twenty-one senses, and possibly more. So, it isn't out of the realm of possibility that a sense of wonder exists.

Once I started doing some research, I discovered a pivotal book published in 1965 called *The Sense of Wonder* by Rachel Carson. In it, Carson recounts her experiences with her nephew and, much like my observations of my own children, concludes that a sense of wonder is something to be cherished, developed, and celebrated.

It wasn't until a recent trip to the beach that I truly understood Carson's words. After a tiring eleven-hour drive to the Outer Banks of North Carolina, we made it to our destination with three wide-eyed children in tow: my two children, Gigi and Camilla, and my eighteen-month-old niece.

The experience began not unlike any other. My children sprinted to the ocean, dipping their toes in the chilly water before belly flopping into the foamy, waist-deep waves. My niece, on the other hand, was a tad more apprehensive. The texture of the squishy, wet sand checked her balance, causing her to take special care with each tiny step.

Of course, I had my cell phone handy and was filming everything, hoping to catch a hint of what exactly this sense of wonder is. Then, all three children circled around something oddly beautiful on the shore. I put my phone back in the beach bag, and we surrounded this viscous bubble of goo. My natural adult instinct was to exercise caution. Could this thing sting, bite, or harm us? But it sure was beautiful. It had an iridescent glow of cotton-candy colors in the sunlight, and it bounced slightly with the gentle pressing of the wind.

We prodded it a bit with seashells before one of the children accidentally stepped on it, and then we realized it wasn't dangerous. But what could it be? Camilla determined it was from a mermaid, and I liked that idea because, truthfully, I had no idea what it was. Gigi, whose favorite hobby is creating doll houses from old Amazon boxes, wondered if it would make a beautiful new chair for her latest cardboard creation.

(margin handwriting: ✱ wonder — but is this possible)

It was a perfect day. Eighty degrees with a light breeze. The ocean was bright blue, and the waves made a calming white noise that lulled in the background. And here I was sitting in the sand with a smile plastered on my face.

That was it.

In that moment, I tapped into my childhood sense of wonder. After that experience, I went back to the brainstorm sheet Ashley, Abby, Staci, and I share, and realized we had already narrowed down many of the elements of wonder from our own experiences in the classroom: the surprise to marvel at something you didn't expect, the curiosity to discover something you didn't know, the freedom to explore something you are interested in, and the inspiration to create something you envisioned.

Through this experience, we realized something rather revolutionary: adults can experience wonder, too. Who better to learn how to rediscover a sense of wonder than teachers? Teachers who can create wonder-filled classrooms for their students. Teachers who can guide students to develop their own sense of wonder.

In the words of Rachel Carson, children need "the companionship of at least one adult who can share [their wonder], rediscovering with [them] the joy, excitement and mystery of the world we live in."

Let that person be you.

WHAT IS WONDER?

It should come as no surprise that the first significant definition of wonder takes us to a school. But in order to discover wonder here, we have to travel back in time to 369 BCE to find one of the most famous teachers the world has ever seen. We imagine him hunched over a desk, reed pen in hand, carefully writing the foundation of wonder as we know it today.

That person is none other than Plato. In his work *Theaetetus*, Plato invents a conversation between the great Socrates, a math teacher, and a bright young student named Theaetetus. Attempting to define knowledge, the men happen upon something even more valuable to us: wonder.

Theaetetus exclaims, "By the gods, Socrates, I am lost in *wonder* when I think of all these things." To which Socrates replies, "This feeling of wonder shows that you are a philosopher, since wonder is the only beginning of philosophy."

Coming back to the modern day, we can make a valuable connection between philosophy and wonder in light of Benjamin Bloom's 1956 taxonomy for the cognitive domain and its 2001 revision by Anderson and Krathwohl. These domains emphasize the importance of higher-order thinking skills: analyzing, evaluating, and creating. Philosophy requires deep, high-level thinking, like those skills at the top of the taxonomy—the type of thinking we expect from philosophers like Socrates and Plato.

If we want our students to flourish as deep thinkers capable of analyzing, evaluating, and creating, then as Plato wrote, "Wonder is the beginning."

Wonder is the beginning of wisdom, and the elements of wonder we're going to cover in this book are synonyms for the very words you'll find in Bloom's taxonomy. The actions related to these elements—reflecting, discovering, exploring, and creating—sound pretty similar to Bloom's higher-order thinking actions, don't you think?

Ironically, it is children who are in tune with their sense of wonder. As Carson explains, "A child's world is fresh and new and beautiful, full of wonder and excitement. It is our misfortune that, for most of us, that clear-eyed vision, that true instinct for what is beautiful and awe-inspiring, is dimmed and even lost before we reach adulthood."

ME: Don't want to lose wonder!

★ 5 ★

Still, dictionaries try to help us by adding hard and fast rules. The words "surprise" and "admiration" (or synonyms of these words) show up in most internet definitions of "wonder." Despite being self-proclaimed wordsmiths (sorry, that's the English teacher in us), we'd prefer not to nitpick word choice.

Rather, we want you to feel it. Think about a time when something truly took your breath away. Maybe it was a beautiful painting at a museum, a stolen kiss, a touching song, a stunning landscape. Whatever it is for you, think about that moment. How did it make you feel? What surprised you about it? What did you think about? These are the "aha" moments we define as wonder, the moments we want both you and your students to relish, the moments we've experienced in our own classrooms.

And if you're still wondering about Jenna's encounter at the beach, good. We've done our job.

After some research, we discovered that the clear blob on the beach was the harmless husk of a dead moon jelly!

HOW WE GOT STARTED AND OUR MISSION

*Ashley

In her book *Big Magic,* Elizabeth Gilbert describes a theory that ideas are living, breathing, wandering things that search the universe for the perfect host to manifest them in the world. Though this theory seems fantastical, it is the only explanation I have for how Keeping the Wonder got started. I never intended to start a workshop. My career plan never included delivering professional development. In fact, I wasn't even thinking about anything education-related when the idea sprung from the ether of the internet and planted so deeply into my brain that I couldn't let it go.

I was leisurely reading my favorite home design blog, *Young House Love*, when a post caught my eye. It read: "Kids Room Ideas from the Cutest Kids Bookstore Ever." From the moment the images appeared on my screen, my eyes grew wide, my jaw slackened, and I stared in awe. The Story Shop in Monroe, Georgia, is in fact the cutest bookstore ever (believe us, we've since done a ton of research trying to match our first and dearest location for a Keeping the Wonder Workshop). Owner Melissa Music and designer Stephanie Cannon dreamed up this bookstore to capture the imagination, creativity, and wonder of children and the books they read. As if I had stepped through my computer screen, across the threshold of the Story Shop's wardrobe, and into the room of possibilities, I knew in an instant that I wanted to plan something to honor the magic of this extraordinary bookstore.

Like any enamored host flirting with an idea, I became obsessed. I stalked images. I researched the town. I typed, overthought, and abruptly deleted multiple messages to the owner. And when the idea didn't wane, I let my mind wonder "What if . . . " Finally, I hit send on a message, but I communicated in such a vague and uncertain way that it would have been easy to ignore or decline. I think I secretly wished someone of authority would shut me down. Why did this idea come to me? Wasn't there anyone else much more qualified? But her response was almost immediate: "Sure! What type of workshop did you have in mind?"

What I had in mind was this: I wanted to create a workshop that would help educators bring back and keep the wonder in education, a workshop that reminded educators how magical the act of learning is supposed to be. A workshop that gave educators the permission and standards-based evidence to make learning fun.

And so, with permission granted from the universe, I brainstormed a few other educators whose teaching philosophy resembled my own: Abby, Jenna, and Staci, all fellow high school English teachers at the time. I only knew them through a collection of squares and stories on Instagram, but I could tell that they were the type of teachers wild enough to say yes to planning a workshop in a month, all while teaching full-time. Thankfully, my hunch was right, and the universe had my back. Compelled by this magical idea, all miraculously agreed, messaging me back agreeing to "do this workshop thing!" And that workshop thing we did. In just a few weeks, we planned and hosted our first Keeping the Wonder Workshop at the quirkiest, cheeriest, dreamiest, and, yes, cutest bookstore ever.

We have since put on several other workshops in magical venues around the US, but the Story Shop will always hold a special place in our hearts. The energy in the room was palpable, and we have each bottled up bits of the magic of that day to carry with us throughout our careers. That magic is with us now in this book. You see, when the universe sends you an idea as electric as this one, you have to do everything in your power to grow it into its entire potential.

Somewhere along the way, education has lost some of its luster. Much like a sweep of Dolores Umbridge through Hogwarts, mandates, scripts, and regulations have dampened the magic of education and snuffed out the wonder in students. We are on a mission to help educators put the sparkle back into standards and the wonder back into work. You are here because you heard the call, and we're so glad you answered.

THE MAGIC MINDSET

Teaching is the most important job in the world, but it can also be a world of fun when you let it. To embrace the strategies in this book, you must first get comfortable with holding a paradox in your head: to be a seriously good teacher, you can't take yourself too seriously! Though education will save the world, the world won't stop when a lesson flops. Though one year with you can change the entire trajectory of a child's life, one misunderstood concept won't ruin their chances for success. You can be both academic and absurd at the same time. Professional and unpredictable. Diligent and delightful. Serious and surprising. Wise and wonder-filled.

EMBRACE A TOOTING LLAMA

As a type A teacher, I crave routine and often become so set in my habits that it would take a spy only twenty-four hours to know my entire schedule. Therefore, as much a surprise to me as anyone who knows my predictable personality, I found myself on an impromptu hike with a llama and a group of sundry yogis. Because of some serendipitous scrolling the evening before, I spotted an advertisement for a llama-trekking and mountaintop yoga event in my area scheduled for the very next day. Something (probably the cute llama faces) compelled me to sign up, so I did.

As my yoga-mat-toting llama and I hiked through the Smoky Mountains on a crisp and colorful fall day, I felt such a sense of adventure and self-importance. I thought, "Look at me being spontaneous! Look at what a serious yogi I am! Look at me living in the moment!"

Once our group of llamas and hikers reached the top of the mountain, the feeling of significance only intensified. As the llamas quietly rested, our yoga instructor softly brought our intention and focus to the magic of the woods and the presence within us. It was all very transcendent, mystical, and serious—until, in a silent moment of meditation, Flash, the lead trekking llama, let out a long, laborious, rambling, and repulsive fart. The spell had broken.

Now, there are a few ways to look at a surprise llama fart in the middle of a woodland yoga haven:

1. Be agitated that the llama's toot ruined the seriousness of a costly yoga retreat.
2. Ignore the llama toot and attempt to regain focus.
3. Giggle at the llama toot like a twelve-year-old.
4. Embrace the llama toot and thank it for the reminder to not take yourself too seriously.

I had engineered an element of surprise and a canvas for wonder by attending something completely out of the norm, but no one could have expected or planned for a llama fart at the most inopportune moment. It was hilarious and ridiculous and bizarre and wonderfully surprising.

This is how engineering wonder works. You plan learning surprises for your students, and you embrace the surprises that come unplanned. You set up your classroom for wonder, and you rediscover wonder for yourself. Surprises and moments of wonder, in their nature, pause the autopilot of our brains and direct our attention to the present. After the surprise, our brains get to work. Schema is activated, learning intensifies, and memory is enhanced.

I had many deep thoughts during this inspirational hike and yoga outing, but as you can tell by this anecdote, the fortuitous flatulence in the middle of meditation, er, lingered with me the longest. Though I'll admit that I did giggle like a twelve-year-old up on that mountain, taking a moment to embrace the llama toot gave me some important educational insight.

When you let go of some of the weightiness of teaching, it allows your brain to frame each lesson with the lens of experimentation. Instead of sticking with a comfortable concept of how school is supposed to look, think of ways you can de-school it. Make teaching and learning an experiment in which the goal of your experimentation is to spark wonder for your scholars in the now, so they can continue to develop their sense of wonder as lifelong learners. Some of the strategies in this book might not work well with your learners. That's okay! Get comfortable with the uncomfortable feeling of uncertainty. Try again. Get creative.

The beauty of teaching as an experiment is that it's all about growth. When your expectation is that you're discovering what works best for your scholars, you won't have "failures." Rather, you'll have an experiment to keep adjusting until you get it right. Like you, the four of us experiment each and every day, because every day is a new learning experience and a chance to get it just right. Like our scholars, we never stop learning because teaching *is* learning.

We wrote this book to guide your experimentation, to give you the ingredients to a successful potion of wonder.

As we work to create joyous classrooms for all students, we invite you to join us on this journey. In this book, you'll explore the elements of wonder so that you can use them to open windows and doors to the magic of learning.

To guide us along the way, we'll be inspired by Rudine Sims Bishop's magical view of reading:

> Books are sometimes windows, offering views of worlds that may be real or imagined, familiar or strange. These windows are also sliding glass doors, and readers have only to walk through in imagination to become part of whatever world has been created and recreated by the author. When lighting conditions are just right, however, a window can also be a mirror. Literature transforms human experience and reflects it back to us, and in that reflection we can see our own lives and experiences as part of the larger human experience. Reading, then, becomes a means of self-affirmation, and readers often seek their mirrors in books.

Just as we hope to provide mirrors, sliding glass doors, and windows in our classrooms, we hope that this book serves you similarly. We hope that you will see yourself in the experiences of other educators, and that this new experimentation will take you on a journey.

On this quest, we'll collect the four elements of wonder: surprise, curiosity, freedom, and inspiration. Each of these elements is one part of the potion to help us make learning magical. But, the final (and most important) ingredient is *you*.

In this book, you'll find our best tips, tricks, strategies, and research, but we also want you to get a view beyond our four classrooms to see these elements put to use in Wonder Classrooms. Throughout the book, you'll be welcomed into our classrooms as well as those of expert Wonder Makers from near and far. In all, you'll have a window into classrooms big and small, public and private, urban and rural. Our hope is that by including these learning environments, you'll be able to open the window to the potential magic in your unique circumstance.

ELEMENT 1

SURPRISE

*Jenna

The moment I stepped over the threshold, I was transported into a wild jungle.

The cement walls became towering green trees, the suspension ceiling became a tangle of low-hanging vines, and the blue area rug became a rushing river ready to take me on a journey to magical learning.

Like Lucy stepping through the magical wardrobe to discover Narnia, I stepped through the door to Mrs. Bakuhn's second-grade classroom.

All of these years later, I can recall the surprise of seeing her classroom jungle for the first time. I was in awe. There was a thick withered tree trunk in the middle of the room complete with sprawling branches and bright green leaves and a howler monkey hanging from one of the vines. Never mind they were made of paper and stuffing. To me, it was *magic*.

The surprise of that day marked only the first of many surprisingly wonderful experiences in my second-grade classroom: the day I sat in our special reading tent for our independent reading time, the day we were explorers at the Pittsburgh Zoo, the day we traveled deep under the sea during our *20,000 Leagues Under the Sea* read aloud, and the day we sang "Baby Beluga" while we learned about beluga whales.

It's no mystery why, despite being only eight at the time, I can still remember so much about that school year. Mrs. Bakuhn knew something magical about learning. She had discovered the first element of wonder: surprise.

★ ★ ★

There aren't too many situations in which we can imagine grown adults ready and willing to crouch under tables or slide behind bookshelves with hushed tones and dimmed lights. But we're guessing you've experienced or at least observed the classic birthday surprise at least once in your life.

We love bursting out of our hiding spots with a hearty "SURPRISE!" to unsuspecting friends on their birthdays, and we love even more the exhilarated "you got me!" surrender when the surprise has played out for them.

We've all had experience with the excitement that comes from a big surprise. When was the last time you were surprised? It's probably not hard to remember a truly exciting surprise because, quite frankly, surprises are *memorable*.

Surprises create wonder.

Psychologists call this phenomenon "flashbulb memory." Coined in 1977 by researchers Roger Brown and James Kulik, a flashbulb memory is a distinct memory created by an emotional disruption in someone's normal routine. Brown and Kulik studied national and global events that impacted people on a large scale, and the results explain why we can remember seemingly trivial details of a big surprise party that occurred three years ago, but can't remember what we ate for lunch two days ago.

Care to give it a try? Think of a special day in your life. Here are some examples:

- The day you found out you got your first teaching job
- The day you graduated from college
- The day you met your partner
- The day your child was born

Chances are you can recall surprising details about that day. Can you remember what you were wearing, who you called on the phone, what you ate? It's pretty surprising, isn't it? Especially considering how easy it is to forget what you did two days ago, let alone two weeks. Need further evidence? Here's a sweet example from Abby's childhood.

Sometimes surprise is as sweet as the first taste of sprinkle-topped ice cream on a crisp summer night. Sometimes, surprise is ice cream— or at least that's how the story of one of my most delightful flashbulb memories from my childhood goes:

It's a sweet summer evening, and just as the fireflies begin to light up the sky, my Very Unreasonable Mother calls us inside from our barefoot game of hide-and-seek. Right on cue, we protest this early bedtime, pleading with our mom: "But it's *SUM-MER!*" After much protest, we reluctantly pull on our pajamas, brush our teeth, and stomp our way into our bedrooms. "You're not even going to read us a book?" we ask incredulously, as our mother betrays us by shaking her head no. Denied our beloved books, my sister and I furiously whisper from our bunk beds after the traitors we call our parents tuck us in. Fifteen minutes later, just as we're about to give up the fight and attempt to actually sleep, we are alarmed by a ridiculous clatter of banging pots and pans.

First, we hear the racket, then the familiar creaks that signal someone is walking up the stairs. Then comes the unexpected sing-song voice of my mom: "Get out of your beds and get into the van! We're getting ice cream!"

We shoot up from our beds in utter delight and astonishment. "Wait, really?" we ask in surprise, as we realize our parents aren't joking. *We're really getting ice cream!* Soon enough, my mom and dad are loading all five of us kids into our minivan, and we're on our way to get a good, old-fashioned ice cream cone. As we try to race the heat melting our cones, we can't stop laughing and replaying that joyful moment when our bedtime sentence turned into a sweet treat.

I'll never forget that night. To this day, my siblings and I still love to spontaneously swerve into McDonald's drive-throughs just for a little taste of that childhood nostalgia. My parents paid less than five dollars for fifty-cent cones for our entire family that night, but the sheer surprise was priceless.

* * *

As you can see, it makes sense that formal definitions of surprise reveal words like "amazement," "marvel," and, of course, "wonder," which pop up in partnership with words like "unexpected" and "sudden." In their book *Surprise: Embrace the Unpredictable and Engineer the Unexpected*, Tania Luna and LeeAnn Renninger provide a fascinating look at how the element of surprise can help us harness these words to grow and learn. They argue that we need to abandon the negative feelings associated with the unknown and unexpected to thrive in a life filled with wonder.

The good news is that teachers were embracing this principle long before Luna and Renninger wrote their book, and for good reason. Learning by surprise is a concept that psychologists and educators alike have studied for years. In fact, researchers often use the word "novelty" to describe this learning mechanism. When something novel or unexpected happens within the familiar context of your classroom, your students are more likely to remember those events—just as we're more likely to remember that surprise birthday party.

Let's take David Johnson, a math teacher from Wisconsin, as an example. Some forty years before Luna and Renninger's book, Johnson was one of the first educators to specifically identify the element of surprise as an effective classroom technique.

"Is the element of surprise present in your classroom NOW? I believe the *element of surprise* belongs there!" Johnson declared.

NO

only in a fire alarm

Aimee E. Stahl and Lisa Feigenson, researchers from Johns Hopkins University's Department of Psychological and Brain Sciences, conducted an interesting study that supports Johnson's assertion. They looked at how eleven-month-old babies react to the element of surprise. By revealing a ball in an unexpected way, like rolling it off a table without dropping or moving it through a wall, they tested the babies' reactions. Babies could be seen rolling, pounding, and squishing the "surprise" ball, which resulted in more engagement, discovery, and most importantly, effective learning.

Dr. Judy Willis, a neurologist and middle school teacher, closes the gap between the laboratory and the classroom. In her book, *Research-Based Strategies to Ignite Student Learning*, she encourages teachers to utilize surprise:

> Use surprise to bring students' brains to attention. Consider employing the technique of surprise to light up students' brains and illuminate the pathways to memory storage. Starting a lesson with an unanticipated demonstration or having something new or unusual in a classroom will spark student attention and curiosity. It can be anything from playing a song as they enter to greeting them in a costume. If students sense novel experiences from demonstrations, descriptions, anecdotes, or even the enthusiasm in their teacher's voice, they will be more likely to connect with the information that follows.

In this section, we're going to highlight our favorite actionable ideas, or "flashbulbs," as we like to call them, to use the element of surprise to engage students' sense of wonder. As you've already learned, novelty leads to learning because it's, well, novel. Therefore, we want you to keep in mind that the ideas and lessons in this section should be a novelty in your classroom as well as your lesson planning.

If you try to incorporate *all* of these particular ideas every single day, they'll lose their luster. Therefore, we are going to share many different ways you can add a spark of surprise. The strategies in this section provide a range of preparation complexity. We think a combination of these ideas is best, but there is no right or wrong way to incorporate them in your classroom. You can always start small and work your way up, and we bet you'll be *surprised* by the results!

CHAPTER 1

FLASHBULB CLASSROOMS

One of the most basic ways that we can harness the element of surprise is through classroom setup. There's nothing like the first day of school when students walk into your room for the first time.

A simple search on Instagram or Pinterest reveals hundreds of pictures and blog posts for classroom decor and design inspiration. During that search, chances are you'll find Staci's magical classroom—and for good reason. Staci's is unlike any classroom we've ever seen. Which is why, with a quick Google search of keywords "Staci Lamb" and "Hogwarts," you'll find her classroom tour on websites like the *Huffington Post, Inside Edition,* and BuzzFeed. Her Harry Potter–themed room is the epitome of surprise! Ivy-and-stone wallpaper in the hallway leads into the room, which is furnished with wooden tables, a couch, and big, comfy chairs. Candles hanging from the ceiling, portraits adorning the walls, and a candle wax warmer filling the room with a seasonal scent are just some of the minor details that make students say, "Wow!" Clearly, Staci has a special gift for decorating, and it pays off in her classroom!

However, you don't have to be a wizard to set up your classroom to harness the element of surprise. We know the idea of decorating can be extremely stressful and overwhelming (we've all been there!), so let us start by simplifying the process for you.

You do *not* have to spend your whole summer decorating, and you do *not* need to spend a lot of money—unless of course you want to do that, and if so, that's fine too! However, we do think there are some things you should consider because students can be distracted by visually overstimulating classrooms. Planning with purpose is our mantra.

Let's break down our recommendations for planning our classroom design with purpose. When thinking about classroom design, here are the questions we ask ourselves:

1. Does it serve an academic, instructional, or organizational purpose?
2. Does it support learning, engagement, collaboration, representation, and/or movement?
3. Is it feasible?
4. Is it worth the time and energy to add it to my classroom?

If you're deliberate with your design, you can surprise your scholars with a student-centered space that maximizes the wonder of learning!

At its core, surprise is simply a disruption of pattern. Whether this disruption is small (having a curious picture projected on the board instead of your normal agenda) or big (turning your classroom into a castle), it will be just enough to grab students' attention and issue an extra dose of dopamine to their brains, which will trigger stronger connections and lead to better long-term memory. In order to uncover, process, and store new information, it's essential to activate the brain's hippocampus. In their study on the effects of novelty on memory, researchers Daniela Fenker and Hartmut Schütze show that novel stimuli (surprises) activate the hippocampus more than familiar stimuli. Therefore, not only are surprises fun to plan and receive, but they are also academically sound.

A ONE-HUNDRED-YEAR-OLD SOFA IN THE MIDDLE OF A TWENTY-FIRST-CENTURY CLASSROOM

Ashley

I love interior design (remember how Keeping the Wonder got started!), and I love bringing my personal passion into classrooms. After doing some research on flexible seating, I decided that I would test it out with a small section of my classroom. I made a plan and then went on the hunt for the perfect sofa to add to my room. I love shopping at thrift stores and antique shops because, unlike online or big-box shopping where you expect to find the exact thing you are looking for, second-hand shops leave lots of room for surprise! Most of the time I won't find anything worth buying, but every so often I will come across the most delightful treasure.

That was the case for the cheery yellow Victorian sofa I found at an antique shop for fifty dollars. It was in pristine condition, and I knew that the sturdy craftsmanship would withstand the use of rowdy teenagers. I later found two pink wingback chairs to flank the sofa and created a makeshift living room right in the middle of my otherwise traditional classroom.

The classroom living room didn't cost much, but the reactions were priceless. No one expects to see a Victorian sofa in the middle of the classroom. Classrooms are for desks: Desks in rows. Desks in rows. Desks in rows. Victorian sofa. Desks in rows. Desks in rows. It disrupted the pattern and delighted the students!

While I knew the sofa and chairs would be a hit, I didn't expect the other lessons and takeaways that came from this classroom setup. Since our classroom living room would only comfortably fit five teenagers, I let my students decide the fairest way to share. On the first day of school, one of my back-to-school stations was set up in the living room area, where I prompted students to discuss the flexible seating and come up with a plan for how we should best use it.

I had some clever and funny suggestions, but the majority voted in favor of taking turns. So, based on student input, I made a classroom rule that each day of the week would be one group's day to choose the living room area if they wished. For example, each Monday, table one had first dibs at the living room area. They almost always took their turn, but if not, the living room was open to first come, first served (the second most popular suggestion from students). Tuesday would be table two's turn, and so forth.

When I did my end-of-semester survey, I asked students to leave a comment about what they thought of the classroom living room. Students wrote:

"I liked that it changed up the week. Made me look forward to Wednesdays a little more!"

"I loved it when I forgot it was my day for the armchair [and] then suddenly remembered when I walked in!"

In other words, an already incongruous one-hundred-year-old sofa in the middle of a twenty-first-century classroom not only surprised and delighted our classroom community on the very first day, it continued to break routine throughout the entire semester!

The classroom living room also created a platform for me to quickly arrange other surprises and activities. For instance, when I wanted to use a picture book to scaffold a concept, I would perch my chair in the living room and have my not-so-pint-size teenagers gather around on the sofa and rug like kindergartners. Imagine their surprise when I told them it was time for a picture book in senior English class! I also continued to use the living room as a center when I implemented stations throughout the year. I always made sure to set up that station as the discussion piece because students loved that "fancy coffee shop" feeling as they gathered around on hip furniture and talked about literature and writing. And in yet another example, students were always quick to use pieces from the living room as props for the mini plays we put on during our drama unit.

★ ★ ★

You will be surprised by how much inspiration will come from adding just one element of surprise to your classroom, but if you can't put a living room in the middle of your space, think of other ways you can disrupt a pattern!

Sparking surprise can be as simple as switching up your desk or table arrangement, so that when your students walk in the classroom, they're caught off guard by a new setup. It's amazing how surprised they are when they see your classroom set up in a new way.

Where will I sit? What's the new activity?

As students trickle in, watch the surprise unfold. Watch how the new seating arrangements affect the energy, discussion, collaboration, and learning in the room.

Can you arrange your desks in a circle, so that students feel equal, and everyone can be easily seen and heard? This is the setup for a Socratic seminar (more on that later) but it can also offer a spontaneous dose of surprise for a regular lesson.

What about arranging your desks in pairs, facing each other? This works perfectly for think-pair-shares, partner work, or one-on-one discussions.

Whether you want to arrange your desks in a circle, a horseshoe, pairs, groups, rows, or islands, you don't have to have a reason. Surprise—if only for a day or two—is worth it. Even if you don't have your own classroom or can't rearrange desks, there are other ways to disrupt the pattern of your classroom environment to surprise your scholars.

Hello. Hello. Hello. Welcome to the Poetry Café, here's your menu. Hello. Hello.

If you greet students the same way each day, say something special or silly that's related to your lesson to mix it up. It will surprise them at the door and keep them guessing until you start your spoken-word unit, for instance.

Silence. Silence. Silence. Jazz music. Silence. Silence.

If you rarely use music in class, then suddenly blast jazz from the Harlem Renaissance, students will take note and be much more tuned in to your lesson on Prohibition or Harlem Renaissance poetry.

Agenda. Agenda. Agenda. Creepy forest sounds. Agenda. Agenda.

Project a daily agenda every day, then don't. Instead, have students walk into a dimly lit room with creepy ambient forest sounds playing in the background for a lesson on creating mood or suspense. Students will be immediately surprised by how different your room feels and intrigued to learn what it's about. If you have a lesson plan, there's ambient media for that. From farm sounds to city rhythms, violent storms to peaceful seas, just search themes related to your content plus the keywords "ambient sounds," and you can create a surprising classroom transformation in under thirty seconds.

Staci

Like Ashley, I have been on many adventures to find classroom furniture, and I especially love a good deal and all the fun that goes into the planning and decorating of my classroom.

For many teachers, getting our own classroom with creative freedom to decorate is a way for us to showcase our interests and who we are as educators. In that same regard, we have to be mindful of whether our decor is reflective of our students as well.

When we walk into a room, part of the surprise is that initial reaction to our environment and our sensory responses to the music, the lighting, and the seating, but an even greater surprise can be walking into a room and seeing ourselves represented there.

Classroom design works much the same way as Bishop's approach to literature. We have to reflect and ask these questions, among many:

- Can students see themselves?
- Can they see others?
- Can they have the opportunity to learn about others through the design?
- Do they have a role in the design?

Our design is not limited to just the furniture we have, but includes everything, from the posters on our walls to the books on our shelves.

Throughout high school, I saw myself, a white woman, in many classrooms and books, but it wasn't until college when I read the assigned text *Fingersmith* by Sarah Waters that I thought, "Are we actually reading a book with LGBTQ+ themes and characters written by an actual LGBTQ+ writer?" The surprise I felt was exciting, yet equally concerning. Had I really made it through more than twelve years of schooling without truly seeing myself fully represented in the curriculum?

Despite the fact that it was a crime novel set in Victorian-era Britain, and I was very much a millennial sitting in a college in Delaware, I connected to this story. I also connected to my teacher for including this book in her curriculum, for fostering our conversations, and for making an effort to be inclusive in the design of her course.

After having my Harry Potter–themed classroom for two years, I made and continue to make changes to the design of my room. I have sought out resources like Project LIT and FirstBook.org to find books that represent various identities and lived experiences and have them displayed all around my classroom. There are books on the window counter, the whiteboard ledge, various bookshelves, on tables, and in baskets. I even have a shoe rack with books on it. Instead of my students looking around and seeing just Harry Potter, I wanted them to have the experience of seeing themselves and others represented in the room.

For posters, I often go to amplifier.org, or I design my own. Amplifier updates its collections of posters often, and even has a special program for teachers to get more free artwork, lesson plans, and other teaching resources.

★ ★ ★

Reflecting on our classroom design should be a process we engage with often. This reflection can happen on your own, but a great way to get students involved is to conduct a survey at the beginning of the year and follow up throughout the year. Ask them about their perceptions of your classroom, what they would change, what they notice, what they like, etc. When you work together to create, change, and adapt the design, it leads to an even better one.

CHAPTER 2

FLASHBULB PROPS

Worksheet. Worksheet. Worksheet. Sidewalk chalk. Worksheet. Worksheet.

Sometimes, adding a novel surprise to your classroom environment can be as simple as changing up the medium in which students are allowed to show or create their work. Think of ways you can surprise students by breaking away from their traditional method of note-taking, annotation, or formative assessment. For example, have them write on sidewalks, leaves, plates, sticky notes, giant paper, desks, dry erase boards, page protectors, windows, boxes, mural templates.

These ideas are flashbulb props. Flashbulb props are new and surprising items to use during a lesson. You can introduce these props before, during, or after a lesson or activity. The surprise comes from an item students didn't expect, and again, this doesn't have to be time-consuming or costly. Here are some other ideas:

- Fancy pens or pencils
- Invisible ink pens (found on Amazon) ??

- Classroom microphones
- Tealight candles (from Dollar Tree) for setting the mood
- Special paper (colored, textured, patterned, rolled, folded)
- Music (playing in the background or incorporated into the lesson)

Jenna

Among my favorite flashbulb props are our Keeping the Wonder Workshop "quill pens." Ashley found these pens on Amazon, and they were a hit at our 2019 workshops, so I decided to purchase a classroom set. What's great about these pens is that I will be able to use them year after year to spark a little surprise. When we started our sonnet unit, I rolled up students' worksheets and added a quill pen to each place setting.

They were *so* excited about these pens! Who would have thought that a simple pen would spark such surprise and engagement? They couldn't wait to write—wait for it—sonnets (yes, sonnets!) with their new quill pens. When this activity is over, I make sure to put them away for another day. Remember, if I kept them out, their novelty would wear off. Now, whenever I do pull them out, it's a surprise.

Abby

One simple prop that will help you spice up the drabbest of lessons is a fun classroom microphone. It's perfect for those days when you quickly realize your lesson isn't the most exciting (it happens!) and you want to compensate for the content with a dramatic delivery. Play reporter and "interview" students with questions about the "breaking news" you are teaching them! Embellish a flopping classroom discussion by letting the students "pass the mic" when they speak. Give students the chance to deliver a presentation with the microphone, too—just don't let them literally "drop the mic!"

Staci

I'm a fidgeter. For as long as I can remember, I have needed something to fidget with, whether it was pencil erasers, my phone clip, magnets, earring backings, or now, my teacher lanyard. It's not uncommon for my fidgets to become an unexpected prop in my lesson. My students see me playing with whatever object I can find, and then for some reason, it becomes intriguing to them as well. So, I started using this to my advantage.

Sometimes, speaking in front of others (such as during group presentations or completing problems on the board) can be intimidating and nerve-racking, and that's where props can save the day. One day, as I was teaching, I grabbed my spooky skeleton hands from Dollar Tree to point at the board and teach, and that was all I needed to do. From there, the students wanted the spooky hands, so anytime someone would talk, they were able to use them!

Ashley

While infamous for being the least desirable classroom in the school, my windowless room has actually never bothered me. It has its perks, to be honest! I never have to worry about weather distractions when other classes go wild at the sight of snow. I have extra wall space for things like epic word walls and student-created murals. And best of all, it gets extra dark for when I want to add an element of surprise! To help embrace my cavernous classroom, I bought an inexpensive star light projector to shine on the ceiling at opportune times. With the click of a button, I can turn my walled-in room into a mystical forest scene, a mysterious night stage, or a mythical book setting. With this projector as a flashbulb prop, I can create surprise and delight that not even a blizzard could match.

CHAPTER 3

FLASHBULB CONTENT

Textbook. Textbook. Textbook. Social media. Textbook. Textbook. While much of what we've discussed involves planning surprises and creating disruptions, sometimes the surprise is already there—right in your content, just waiting for you to find it. This simple version of the surprise element is all about extracting the unusual, odd, or novel from your existing content, whether that's a short story, historical event, or science experiment. As educational researcher Robert Marzano suggests, presenting unusual information is inherently engaging because it disrupts the mind's process of organizing knowledge. Surprising content can be anything that's quirky, unexpected, little-known, or just plain weird. If you can find a surprising nugget of information, an interesting connection, or an almost "too good to be true" example, then sell that to your students and instantly elevate your engagement.

Here are our favorite ways to find flashbulb content:

> **Sudden sounds:** *Does your content relate to sound?* If so, you can engineer surprise by inserting random sounds into your

lesson. Think of it like a classroom prank except you are the prankster! For example, Kwame Alexander is a master at using words to create sound, like in his book *Crossover* when he uses word techniques to mimic pacing down a basketball court and swishing a ball through the net. Before a syntax and sound lesson, discretely play the sound of a basketball dribble getting louder and louder until your students notice. Then, hook them into the lesson by playing other sports sounds and analyzing how those sounds translate into words on the page. Other examples to inspire your sounds include confusing students with the sound of someone whispering during a lesson on the Red Scare, or the mystery sound of a well-known invention before a lesson on the Industrial Revolution. Prick up your ears and an idea will come!

Surprising social apps: *Can you use social media content for a "cool" lesson?* If you're teaching persuasion tactics, logical fallacies, or rhetorical devices, you can surprise students by letting them peruse social media. Give students permission to scroll through Instagram and search for examples of social media marketing. Not only will using their phones for learning be a novel experience, students will be even more surprised to see just how much persuasion is impacting their everyday lives.

Unexpected mediums: *Can you use an unexpected medium to reach a learning goal?* For example, instead of the printed word, could you surprise students with a podcast? Unlike many traditional texts, podcasts provide modern, diverse, expertly produced information and stories that will delight and engage the ears of all learners! Additionally, podcasts expose ELL students to authentic conversational language, while paired transcripts help boost literacy in striving readers.

Unforeseen images: *Can you present surprising visual text pairings?* Using picture books with high school students is one way to nurture their nostalgia and surprise them with complexity. For instance, when teaching rhetorical analysis, pairing Malala Yousafzai's Nobel Prize acceptance speech with her powerful picture book *Malala's Magic Pencil* is a great way to study rhetorical appeals through the spoken word and visual text. Peruse picture books, political cartoons, advertisements, and photography, and you'll be surprised at how many unpredictable pairings you'll find!

Astonishing articles: *Can you find an interesting article that relates to the content?* For instance, you can start the unit with an article on how scientists engineered glow-in-the-dark cats before a unit on genetics. (It's true! Look it up!)

Bewildering language: *Are you reading something like* Beowulf *that has been translated into modern English? Hwæt!* Using a serious tone, you can have students struggle through the strange language, then surprise them with the translation! This will create a learning opportunity for language change and emphatic public reading alike.

Shocking endings: *Are you teaching content that has a surprise ending?* Enhance this feature by building up to the surprise. Have students sign a contract or make a pledge at the beginning of the unit that they won't read ahead or look up spoilers. If they cave, they must promise to keep the secret!

Abby is a big fan of small flashbulb surprises because she loves finding quirky content to "trick her students into learning." Let's look at some of the examples she uses in her classroom.

Abby

When I teach my students about journalistic ethics and the importance of fact-checking, I start with an unusual example of what *not* to do. I pass out copies of the fabricated article "Hack Heaven" by serial liar and former journalist Stephen Glass, and then I facilitate a discussion on the article as if it is true. I treat it like it's any other discussion on an article or current event, and I make sure that the students are invested in the content before I reveal to them that the article is entirely *fake*.

One year, I even printed out ridiculous memes and taped them to the bottom of my students' desks just to make the "you've been punk'd!" moment that much more dramatic. Some laughed, some cringed, and some simply said, "Wait, what?!" but all of them were engaged in that moment of astonishment. Every year, I live for that moment: their expressions, comments, questions, and even their pretend anger toward me.

Another time I sneak in a mini surprise is at the beginning of our poetry unit, when I find song lyrics that sound poetic and poetry that could pass as music! I give students a fun "quiz" that challenges them to differentiate between the poetry and the music. Even the self-proclaimed music enthusiasts miss questions because the lines between poetry and music are blurred. My goal is always to remind them that music is poetry, too, and this simple surprise serves as an engaging hook to our unit.

When you can extract the juicy, unusual content—you know, the stuff that's not in textbooks—you can always find a way to make each lesson more surprising. While each example of flashbulb content might not be totally awe-inspiring, a series of mini surprises over time will add up to create wonder in your classroom.

 Staci

Surprise does not always have to be exciting and full of joy; rather, it can be a revelation, a surprise in the act of wondering about different perspectives. An epiphany that makes you see the world in which we live differently.

I grew in up New Castle, Delaware, and throughout my childhood, I knew many people who were in and out of prison, but I never truly understood the complexities of how the prison system worked or who was most affected by the systems in place. I'll never forget the day I was sitting in my Women and Gender Studies college class when my professor began discussing prison statistics and how people of color and people from low socioeconomic backgrounds are disproportionately represented in those statistics.

It was a surprise to me. A heartbreaking, disappointing one at that, but nonetheless a surprise. It made me wonder. It made me question. It made me want to learn more about what I knew and, more importantly, what I didn't know.

Sometimes in our classrooms, we will have to navigate tough material, maybe even material that we are still learning and unlearning. While we do not want to trivialize this kind of material in the form of quirky activities, we want to allow for these surprises to occur, for reflection to occur, and for dialogue to occur.

Almost ten years after taking that course, I now find myself teaching *Just Mercy*, a nonfiction text by Bryan Stevenson that explores the injustices we see in the judicial system, with a particular focus on marginalized people. Interestingly enough, Stevenson also grew up in Delaware, a fact I often share with my Maryland students.

As we read this book, and other books like it, we discuss, analyze, reflect, and engage with complex material. Even through the simple act of discussion, we learn so much from each other because a natural surprise occurs every time someone speaks.

I often find myself saying to my students, "Wow, I hadn't thought of that before" or "That's a great point. Thank you for sharing your perspective and experiences." To me, those are some of the most profound surprises we get to experience in education.

CHAPTER 4

FLASHBULB ACTIVITIES

Test. Test. Test. Act it out. Test. Test.
We love the idea of giving students a novel activity to show what they know, something exciting and out of the ordinary. An old-school example is a video project that we all remember doing as students ourselves. Back in the early 1990s and early 2000s, we borrowed our parents' camcorders and had to film and re-film one-take videos because we didn't have editing options on VHS and DVD players!

Times sure have changed; our students are now so skilled with video that we're incorporating green screens and iMovie. The point is that we don't do these activities every day, which makes them a fun surprise when they do come along.

Here are some of our favorite flashbulb activities:

- **Video:** Can students create an advertisement, reenactment, summary, interpretation, or skit?
- **Scavenger hunt:** Can students collect items, digitally or in the classroom, that relate to your topic?

- **Book:** Can students collaborate on a collection of writing or create their own book?
- **Act it out:** Can students perform a live skit or vocal acting?
- **Smart art:** Can students use art (drawing, sculpture, painting, etc.) to represent their understanding of a subject?
- **Character interviews:** Can students interview characters or historical figures?
- **Discussions:** Can students participate in a whole-class or small-group discussion?
- **Visual notes:** Can students color, sketch, or visually represent notes?

Staci

Imagine my students' faces the day I told them that within four weeks, they would become published authors. Not too far into the school year we were charged with writing personal narratives, and I began to question, "How can this assignment be as authentic as possible? What can I do to get the most out of my students?"

Barely containing my excitement, I walked into school the next day and surprised them with, "We're writing a book!" I'd love to say that they all stood up, cheered joyfully, high-fived all of their friends, and shouted back, "Yeah! Let's write one!" But let's be realistic: they were teenagers after all, and they had only known me for one month. Who was I to make such a grand claim about what they would and could do? Behind their confused glances to their peers, I saw something, and it was exactly what I had hoped: they were intrigued.

Over the next few weeks, we typed and typed and typed. Edited and edited. Proofread and peer-read. Finally, we compiled their work into a template from Lulu, our publishing website, and named the book *Behind the Door of G115*. After we designed the front cover of the book, which was just a picture of a door from a classroom down the hallway with some text overlay, we submitted the file and waited for the copies of their book. Just three weeks later, a box of books arrived to our classroom, and as I carefully glided the scissors over the packing tape, I could see it on their faces: this was real. Separating them from *their* book was bubble wrap and an invoice. We opened the box of books together, and they immediately looked for their stories.

Shortly after the copies arrived, I reached out to the local newspaper and asked them if they'd be interested in talking with my students. They said yes, and the very next week, the students were photographed and interviewed. One of my kids mentioned that his mom took him out for ice cream as a way to celebrate his accomplishment.

The article garnered some attention for their book, and as a result, we decided to have a book signing in the school library. Our media specialist graciously welcomed us, providing tables and beautiful purple tablecloths for us to use. We had yellow flowers in vases on each table, copies of the book for sale, and signs and posters welcoming school community members. Throughout the day, members from our school and even members from the district's leadership team showed up in support of their work.

Although the newspaper article and book signing were momentous occasions, another driving force behind this work was the financial benefit for the students. They knew from the start of the project that all proceeds would go to them. Each book cost about $2.15 to print, and we sold them for $5. All of the money earned from the online sales went into a checking account through the school, and for the in-person sales, we used a simple process: we had a tracking sheet and cash envelope, and we deposited the money into the account weekly.

Initially, we used the profits to buy more copies of the book so that people did not have to wait for their copies (there's nothing like getting something the minute you pay for it!). To no one's surprise, the students decided to spend the rest of their profits on food and beanbag chairs. Together, we made a shopping list for a huge barbecue at the end of the year, and they were once again recognized for their work.

On the very first page of the book, one of my students wrote, "I'm sitting in my English class right now writing this stupid book. I don't really like typing because I'm not smart enough to do it." Now, you might question, "Why would Staci choose *that* opening line of all lines?" The answer: the surprise at the end of that very same story. After detailing her struggles as a learner, her difficulty in managing her emotions, and her trouble with making friendships, the student ended her story with this:

> This book idea might be stupid to me right now, but in the long run, it could also be a great thing. It could help me talk about things easier with my peers or family so that they understand me better. There is a quote in my teacher's room, and it says, 'Mistakes are proof that you are trying.' I know I can be smart, but sometimes I don't bother trying because I know I'll just mess up. When I don't try, I feel like I'm failing myself. Maybe this book will be something that I don't give up on.

Not only did she not give up on her assignment, she finished her entry. Little did she know that her story would be heard by and impact thousands of people, and that together we would all experience this wonderful opportunity.

This experience was so monumental that in 2020, my students repeated the process. This time, however, we decided to use Amazon to reach a wider audience. Despite the COVID-19 closure, they sold, and continue to sell, hundreds of copies of *What You Don't See*, a collection of stories from the class of 2022–2023.

CLASSROOM DRAMATIZATIONS

Lecture. Lecture. Lecture. Mock trial. Lecture. Lecture.

A dramatization is a play or movie adapted from a novel or depicting a particular incident. Using this definition, we coined the concept "classroom dramatization" to represent a lesson or activity that dramatizes a novel or particular incident. Drama and theater for students have long been touted as effective literacy strategies, but what we mean is more incidental, or surprising, for students.

In a classroom dramatization, the teacher creates a scenario or assumes a role related to the lesson and surprises the students by putting them in the middle of the scenario. This activity can also function as a fresh or out-of-the-ordinary lesson that students have time to practice and prepare.

To give you some inspiration, here are our favorite classroom dramatizations:

- **Mock trial:** *Is something wrong?* Make someone take the stand to defend a situation or event. It can be a character from a book, or something more abstract like greed.
- **Explorers:** *Are you exploring a new idea or topic?* Fill the role of a travel guide and take your students on an excursion to explore new content.
- **Crime scene investigation:** *Are you investigating something?* Challenge your students to solve a case related to your content.
- **Escape or breakout scenario:** *Is there a way you can create an escape task to explore the content?* Create a scenario where students have to break out of or escape your classroom. You can find print-and-go escape rooms on Teachers Pay Teachers or Breakout EDU.

- **Autopsy:** *Are you examining someone or something?* Challenge your students to be medical examiners to explore your content or a character.
- **Surgery:** *Is something broken?* Fix broken grammar, math problems, a science experiment, or a time period in history.
- **Content tasting:** *Are you previewing information or a book?* Invite your students to "taste" new ideas or concepts.
- **Memorial:** *Is a character, historical figure, or concept "dead" or antiquated?* Whether it's dead, overused words or the Great Gatsby himself, ask your students to put it to rest through an engaging memorial.

There's nothing more surprising than transforming your classroom into a courtroom. A mock trial is an engaging, authentic way to trick your students into learning, because what they're really doing is analyzing a text, evaluating evidence, generating and defending claims, anticipating counterarguments, writing an argument, delivering a speech, and actively listening to their opponents.

Sure, you could hit just about the same standards (minus the speaking and listening) by assigning a five-paragraph essay, but a mock trial is more memorable. If you'd like to surprise your students with a memorable learning experience, instead of a mere lesson or assignment, you can take the exact same content and frame it with the intriguing structure of a trial.

Throughout the course of a mock trial, I see struggling readers engaging with a text and making connections. I see quiet students gaining confidence and finding a voice. I see reluctant students breaking their "too cool for school" motto and expressing interest. I see my students coming together to engage in a learning experience that means more than any essay I could ever assign.

But perhaps the best part is the surprised look on their faces when I ask them, "Do you know what we just did?" and they realize they wrote an entire essay in groups . . . without complaining. I tricked them into learning—mission accomplished!

ROOM TRANSFORMATIONS

Familiar. Familiar. Familiar. Transformed. Familiar. Familiar.

Combining many of the above elements leads us to one of our favorite activities: room transformations. In their book, *The Wild Card*, Hope and Wade King define room transformations as "a way to change up the classroom decor to bring students into a new (simulated) environment that will set the mood for and support the content." To give you a truly magical introduction to classroom transformations, we take you to Tanya Diaz's classroom in Miami-Dade County Public Schools. Tanya is a science coach, and we are constantly in awe of her ingenuity.

WONDER MAKER

TANYA DIAZ (@GIFTEDTEACHER305)

"Come one! Come all! Step right up to the Chemistry Carnival!" I bellowed. I opened the classroom door dramatically slow, dressed head to toe as a ringleader, top hat on, Hula-Hoop in one hand, with music blasting in the background. Giddy with excitement, the students walked past me through a golden tinsel curtain, eyes round like quarters as they were met by flashing lights and the aroma of popcorn wafting through the air. They took their seats, all the while whispering to each other, "I don't know what we're doing, but it looks like fun!" "I think we're doing something with chemicals!" and "I can't wait to get started!" The day flew by as the students progressed from station to station like a school of fish in the current of a steady stream. Enthused, they worked collaboratively through challenges involving abstract concepts like chemical changes and energy transfers.

Having taught fifth-grade science for the last nine years, I was confident of the usual student pitfalls. Abstract concepts like force and motion, practice of science skills, and physical and chemical changes always top the list of challenges. Right before the school year began, I made a commitment to make these hard-to-grasp concepts exciting, unforgettable, and accessible for *all* students. But how could I do that? What would I use to hook my students? How could I maintain their focus with subjects they found to be, well, boring? I knew the solution would lie in things they loved: games, costumes, music, technology, and socialization.

Armed with this knowledge, I began my quest for fun, hands-on, thrilling activities that were, and still are, academically rigorous. I wanted to immerse my students in a transformative experience with a hint of the fantastical because, in my opinion, life is always more fun peppered with a bit of theatrical drama. I spent that summer developing standardized activities and practical lessons that reflected real-life experiences. I shopped at flea markets for unique props, wrote grants, and scoured my town for garage sales. I wanted to transform the classroom into a place my students could not wait to enter.

When the school year began, I felt energized and empowered with my new sidekick—classroom transformations! During the ten-month school year, I succeeded in making the classroom a wonder emporium of the imagination. Our classroom transformed into a carnival, a magical potions class, a NASCAR racetrack, a bakeshop, the NFL Super Bowl, and the NBA finals. I was pleasantly surprised to find my students waiting for me at the classroom door long before the morning bell.

Soon after I started the classroom transformations, I realized they were taking on a life of their own as the kids clamored to help me plan and decorate. For some of my students, it was the first time they had a burning desire to succeed at school! Parents who never showed up for school events volunteered to help decorate, donate, and even assist with the classroom transformations.

What is the marvel, the magic, and the wonder of classroom transformations? The answer is simple: understanding your students' passions and interests. These are the gateway to comprehending their needs and empowering your instruction to create astonishing, impactful, and never-ending ripples of knowledge.

As you can see, classroom transformations incorporate many of the flashbulb elements we've already discussed. Like Tanya, you can incorporate flashbulb props, set up a new flashbulb desk arrangement, add flashbulb decor, and of course, set up a flashbulb activity. The best part about a room transformation is that it can be dramatic and theatrical or low-prep and simple! Depending on your goals for the lesson and the time you have available, you can choose as many (or as few) of the elements to add to the magic of the room transformation.

Maybe you're reading a short story and want to turn on the classic YouTube fireplace, switch the lights off, and flip on some battery-powered tealight candles. Or perhaps you want to throw a few flowers and doilies on some desks for a lesson on love sonnets.

Speed Date
Emily
Dee Whitman

For the ultimate room transformation, can you take your students outdoors for a change of scenery and breath of fresh air?

A room transformation can be as simple as some tablecloths, decorative signs, and a fun design on your projector or SMART board. Whether it's a full room transformation or just a tweak, it will be a refreshing change of pace for your students and a chance for you to harness the energy of their surprise during your lesson. We love how Staci describes her experience with classroom transformations.

Staci

One of my favorite genres to read and teach is mystery. I love that sitting-on-the-edge-of-your-seat feeling, and I wanted my students to have just that when they walked into our classroom for the first day of the new unit. As students walked toward my room, they were met with caution tape blocking off the classroom door, the theme song to *Law & Order: Special Victims Unit* filling the hallways, and me, Detective Lamb, standing there armed with my detective sunglasses, FBI badge, and head-to-toe black apparel. I presented my students with the necessary materials to solve the crime that had been committed the previous night in our very own classroom: a manila folder, complete with a press release, evidence tracking sheet, writing organizer, and a report sheet. To gain access to the room, they had to be approved by the fingerprint scanner, which was just a simple application on my phone. Right before they walked into the dark room, I gave them their final piece of equipment: a small flashlight. They had no idea what was waiting for them.

Over the course of three days, my students engaged in an inquiry-based lesson in which they traveled to different stations of a crime scene. They analyzed bloody handprints, knocked-over desks, bandages galore, shoes and clothing, plane tickets, and much more to determine the victims, suspects, clues, and possible scenarios of the crime. They made note of these items, described them in detail, and tried to piece together what the evidence could mean. They discussed ideas with their peers, used their flashlights to look in every box and crevice, and referred to each other as agents.

Although I guided them along the way, they became invested in the lesson and took on the roles and responsibilities necessary to solve the mystery. Every single student was engaged from start to finish. Some of them even rushed back to their seats to write their reports about what they thought happened at the scene of the crime.

During the unit, they would cite strong evidence, produce clear writing, analyze patterns of texts and authors, and acquire new vocabulary, all of which aligned directly to our standards-based goals. Oftentimes, students struggle with the idea of citing evidence from a text to support analysis. When they were given tangible pieces of evidence, such as the clues in the crime scene, they cited that evidence to develop their report. Any time we read texts going forward, I would refer to the crime scene lesson: "Remember how we had to cite appropriate evidence to support the report? Now, do the same, except cite evidence from your novel to support your analysis." The experience granted them the opportunity to form long-lasting memories and connections with the content.

In the following weeks, students presented their stories to the class as we devoured the mystery readings in our unit. Their original material became part of our unit, and we analyzed the elements of a mystery in their stories, any connections to the books, and ways to improve their writing skills.

In this lesson, they were agents. In other lessons, they might be attendees at Romeo's memorial, hippos in a life-size game of Hungry Hungry Hippos, lawyers for the narrator in "The Tell-Tale Heart," or diners at the Punctuation Restaurant. Why? Because a little surprise can go a long way.

★ ★ ★

Staci's example brings all of these flashbulb elements together in an extraordinary yet manageable way, and that really is the key for making surprise magic in the classroom. We definitely do not want to leave you with the impression that room transformations are "go big or go home." So, to wrap up this chapter, we asked our mini-transformation expert, Anisa Khandwalla, to give us some ideas for mini-transformations with big impact. Anisa, a math teacher in Houston with ten years of experience, describes several mini-transformations using flashbulb elements that you can replicate in your classroom.

WONDER MAKER

ANISA KHANDWALLA (◉ @CREATIVEUNDERTAKINGS)

Instagram and Pinterest can be overwhelming places, but they are also bursting with creativity. I've always been big on bringing games and the "wow" factor into my classroom, and social media has helped foster those ideas and inspire more. I love review days in my class, either as a way to prepare for a test or to reinforce the material. They can be mini-transformations, have an element of technology, or just be simple games like Connect Four or Grudgeball.

When it's a test review day, students get a review sheet a few days prior, work it out to the best of their ability, and come to class the day before the test with it completed. I then do activities that take the review questions a step further. In each example, I include some flashbulb prop ideas to fit the theme. Then, I create a review task within that theme. Here are some test review examples that I use in my classroom and you can be inspired to apply to yours.

STRANGER THINGS TEST REVIEW

Here are the props I use for this themed review: a *Stranger Things* poster on the door, a note for kids to be ready to enter "the Upside Down," *Stranger Things*–themed music playing throughout the classroom, and tables grouped into four stations, one for each review question. Then, at each station, I have a review game, such as a scooping game (scooping cotton balls from one bowl to another while blindfolded), a paper puzzle of Eggo waffles (a time-period symbol in the show), ciphered clues related to the show that reveal clues hidden around the classroom, and a string of mini lights with the alphabet (another important symbol from the show) taped to the whiteboard as a clue.

I love the element of a "breakout" using Google Forms, which has students answer one section at a time, getting each correct before moving on. If they have never watched the Netflix show, I provide a quick summary. This is a blended experience with answering questions, doing a physical activity (trivia, puzzle, scavenger hunt, and alphabet light clues), and using Google Forms to self-check. Although you facilitate, the kids will rock it with their teamwork and competitive nature.

DISNEY REVIEW DAY

Here are some flashbulb prop ideas to set the mood for this Disney-themed review day: a Disney outfit, complete with mouse ears, a Disney poster on the door, Disney songs playing throughout the classroom, a Disney tapestry from Amazon, and desks moved into four groups for four themed movie stations.

Students answer four rational-number operation questions per station, then play a game, such as a *Finding Nemo*–themed Let's Go Fishin' game from Five Below, or a *Big Hero 6* bowling game. Students have a blast singing along, working together, and playing the games.

STARBUCKS REVIEW DAY

This is such a simple idea, but one my students rave about the most. I start with a Starbucks cup wreath for my door, a barista-style green apron, green and brown butcher paper for the tables, and lamps and fairy lights. As students come in the door, I ask their name and then change it up to be a little silly, writing it on a small disposable cup.

Students are then put into groups based on what I have projected on my SMART board. They work on an activity to calculate tax and tip for different orders at a café. Once they have finished and agree as a group, they are able to come to the counter and get their free cold mocha with whip (aka chocolate milk and whipped cream. I do send out a letter in advance to make sure there are no allergies and such).

EIGHT WONDERS OF THE WORLD DIGITAL TEST REVIEW

A friend on Instagram who taught me about My Maps with Google inspired this digital breakout test review. This is a really low-prep option that still brings the "wow" factor. All you'll need is Google Maps, Google Forms, and students' devices.

On the premade Google map, students go to ten stops: eight wonders plus two pit stops. At each stop, they read a little bit about the wonder and then solve review problems related to it. They then put their answers in a Google form, which lets them know if they are on the right track or not. The short answer response validation feature is the best thing invented! The validation option in Google Forms kept students from being completely stumped (hints were provided), and it kept them moving without asking a million questions.

Using mini-transformations and breakouts in my class keeps my kids engaged and enthused. I love finding different ways to incorporate movement and communication so students will always leave my class wanting to tell someone else about the day they just had.

CHAPTER 5

FLASHBULB LESSON PLANNING

Obviously, these activities seem like fun and games (because sometimes they literally are both fun and games), but it doesn't have to be a puzzle to plan flashbulb lessons.

For creating a well-designed flashbulb activity, we use a modified Understanding by Design (UbD) approach. Ultimately, our goal is to create standards-based, higher-level thinking activities to engage our students. Therefore, UbD is a backward-design approach that starts with the desired results for students and works backward to create learning opportunities and instruction.

Here are our steps for you to start planning your next flashbulb lesson:

- **Start with your standards.** Identify your standards for the lesson.
- **Define your learning objective(s).** Explain what students will be able to do by the end of the lesson.

- **Develop your learning experience.** This can include any of the classroom dramatization or transformation ideas, or something a bit more traditional like a classroom read-aloud, a discussion, or a writing opportunity.
- **Choose a flashbulb.** Think about how you can incorporate any of the flashbulbs we've previously discussed. Remember Jenna's example? It can be as simple as adding a unique pen to a lesson. Again, it doesn't have to be "go big or go home!"

Lastly, here are a few things to remember as you plan your flashbulbs:

- **Act the part!** Trust us, we are *not* great actors, but we do have a lot of heart, and that goes a long way!
- **Dress the part!** You can almost always piece together a free homemade costume for your role. For example, you can use an old black graduation gown for a judge or borrow a lab coat from the science teacher for an autopsy.
- **Be confident!** When trying something new, it's really easy to fall into the trap of justification where you feel like you need to defend what you're doing to students. But, as you've now learned, there is a solid research base to support the element of surprise in your classroom.
- **Keep trying!** Remember, surprise is spontaneous and imperfect. One idea might flop, but the next could be the lesson that students will never forget. If you keep working at it, you just might end up surprising yourself.

When you see one of those heartwarming stories where an educator has been teaching for thirty-plus years and still loves going to work each day, you will almost always hear this teacher say something along the lines of, "This is the best job in the world. There's never a dull moment!" You can tell by the twinkle in their eye that they really mean it. Even as veteran teachers, they still appreciate the novelty and surprise that teaching brings day after day. They must be the type of teacher who embraces chaos instead of wielding control. The type of teacher who switches things up at a moment's notice to better reach their students instead of sticking to a plan that isn't working. The type of teacher who finds humor, joy, and excitement from the whims of children. The type of teacher who understands that sometimes sorrow, injustice, and pain will shadow their spirit.

The challenge, the uncertainty, and the *surprise* are what keeps teachers like these on top of their game for the entirety of their careers. Dull drains the life out of careers. Dull drains the life out of classrooms. Dull drains the life out of life.

"Never a dull moment" is the stuff of life! Learn to embrace it, because when teachers know how to engineer and enjoy surprise, they are setting themselves up for a lifelong career where they, too, can genuinely say at the end of it, "This is the best job in the world!"

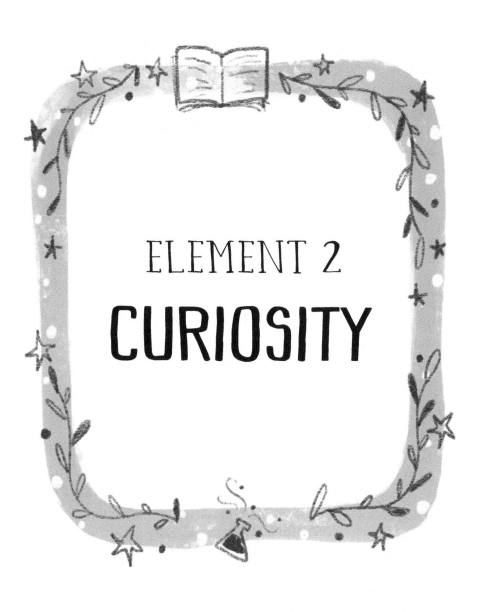

ELEMENT 2

CURIOSITY

The gap

"Mind the gap between the train and the platform!"

Those who've had the delight of visiting or living in the United Kingdom will have read this phrase in a robotic British accent. As a safety precaution, trains in the UK remind travelers to "mind the gap" between the train and the platform before each journey. The goal is for travelers to be mindful while stepping over the gap to board the train to Oxford (or less studious destinations).

In lesson planning, educators should also mind the gap! At its core, curiosity is the act of closing the gap between something we want to know more about and something we have learned. Therefore, it could be argued that the gap is actually the most important element of the entire loop! Love them or loathe them, sites like BuzzFeed and Upworthy have perfected the gap through their headlines. Captions like "You'll never guess which famous book was written on a train!" and "These secret vistas will leave you breathless; find them before the tourists do!" create such an information gap that only the most disciplined individual could resist clicking to learn the answer. How amazing would it be if educators could generate this level of intrigue with their curriculum topics?

If you learn to mind the gap, you can do just that! In fact, it's essential that you do.

It has long been accepted that intelligence (the ability to acquire and apply knowledge and skills) and conscientiousness (the ability to follow academic and societal rules) are the two main predictors of academic performance. However, in a 2011 study titled "The Hungry Mind," researchers performed a meta-analysis from the data of two hundred studies and discovered that intellectual curiosity is the third pillar of academic performance.

Look up?

To continue our analogy, let's revisit the train station. When you picture scholars boarding the train, imagine students taking their seats and waiting in eager anticipation for the cheerful clank of the food trolley rolling up the aisle in their cabin. The hungrier students are, the more anticipation builds. The more they anticipate the selections, the more they will engage with the cart when the attendant finally asks, "Anything from the trolley, my dear?"

Perhaps you are ravenous for research?

Starved for independent study?

Gluttonous for a good story?

Athirst for an academic adventure?

Piggish for perplexing problems?

The goal is to prime students' curiosity so that they are salivating to study. Just like with hunger, people's curiosity satiation can wax and wane based on interests and other factors. But it's important for educators to do their very best to amp up the curiosity appetite of all students, because evidence shows curiosity transcends common achievement gaps.

In a research study of kindergartners, Shah et al. discovered a strong correlation between greater curiosity and greater achievement in reading and math. In their words, "Fostering curiosity may optimize academic achievement at kindergarten, especially for children with low [socioeconomic status]."

Tapping into students' inquisitiveness will not only mind the curiosity gap, but may also help to close the achievement gap. However, while this research is encouraging, it's important to note that curiosity isn't a cure-all for systemic issues in education.

Nevertheless, we should strive to spark, cultivate, and facilitate curiosity to better set up all learners for success. The platform is where your students currently stand on a skill and schema level. What we will call the Wonder Train is the learning journey you wish your students to embark upon. While passengers vary in skill level,

learning ability, work ethic, background knowledge, intrinsic motivation, and socioeconomic status, it's essential to mind the curiosity
gap between the train and the platform so that every student will be
best primed for learning. When you pique the interest of all students,
you level the platform before they climb on board.

CHAPTER 6

DEFINING CURIOSITY

READ TO FIND OUT HOW A ONCE-IN-A-LIFETIME TOUR OF THE SWISS ALPS ENDED IN BLOODSTAIN

Ashley

The train my husband and I were on had just reached the top of a towering Swiss Alp, ascending into a complete whiteout. Once framing Alpine green scenery, the floor-to-ceiling windows of the Bernina Express now revealed only pure white. It was surely still snowing, but I couldn't tell because the whiteout we saw was actually from the ten-foot snow tunnels our steady train was barreling through. We were the only passengers in our cabin who were conversing in English, but during this section of the journey, all multilingual chatter stopped. Snow has a silencing effect, and its peaceful presence was no different on this epic high-altitude ride.

As I stared in wonder at the glittery white blanket that completely engulfed our train, my look of awe quickly turned to one of horror when I glanced over at my husband and saw a bright scarlet stream running down his nose. The red blood was in such startling contrast with the stark white surrounding us that it suddenly felt like every passenger was transfixed by the crimson Americans in the back. To make matters worse, neither of us had anything to stop the nosebleed that rushed down his face like the glacial blue rivers we had crossed at the foot of the Alps.

Fortunately, it turns out that distress and embarrassment are universal languages. A very kind Dutch woman in another row pulled a pack of tissues out of her bag and handed it to my husband while making a hand gesture indicating "keep them all, *please!*" As he held the blood-stained wad of tissues up to his face for the remainder of the four-hour journey, he gurgled, "Couldn't you have just watched a YouTube video?"

★ ★ ★

For the purpose of this chapter, curiosity can be divided into two main categories: diversive curiosity and epistemic curiosity. The difference between the two is the difference between curiously clicking the link "This secluded Swiss railroad is straight out of a fairy tale" and taking a months-researched, awe-inspiring, blood-stained, mountain-scaling, snow-covered, memory-making train journey from Chur, Switzerland, to Tirano, Italy, on the Bernina Express.

According to Ian Leslie's *Curious: The Desire to Know and Why Your Future Depends on It*, diversive curiosity can be described as the attraction to novelty. It's the type of curiosity that lures us into clicking baited headlines. It's the type of curiosity that prompts us to explore odd elements in our environment by touching, smelling, and looking. It's the type of curiosity that satisfies a surface-level need for knowledge. It's the type of curiosity that can be sated with a single click.

On the flip side, Leslie describes epistemic curiosity as a deeper pursuit of inquisitive knowledge. It's the type of curiosity that drives in-depth inquiry. That requires more effort, but has longer-lasting effects. That expands on newness rather than treating novelty as a one-off experience. That spurs an unquenchable desire to keep learning at full steam ahead.

Both diverse and epistemic curiosity mind the information gap between the train and platform, but epistemic curiosity is the deepest form of curiosity and therefore reaps the deepest understanding. To facilitate a deeper form of curiosity, educators like 2020 Arizona Teacher of the Year Lynette Stant can spark curiosity through novel experiences, then cultivate that diverse spark in order to lay the tracks for an epistemic journey of discovery.

WONDER MAKER

LYNETTE STANT (@TEACHINBEAUTY)

THIS LURING PROJECT HAS BUILT-IN CLICKBAIT! READ ON TO GET HOOKED!

Curiosity comes naturally for children; tapping into it and helping students foster curiosity provides an opportunity to trust them to develop and learn in a way that honors their ability to drive their own education. Creating an environment that amplifies a student's ability to ask questions and discover more about their world is the foundation of curiosity.

A standard in our science unit is to "develop and use models to explain that plants and animals (including humans) have internal and external structures that serve various functions that aid in growth, survival, behavior, and reproduction." Though the objective is written in boring educational jargon, my plan to teach it was anything but. You should have seen the excitement in students' eyes when I told them we were going to build crayfish traps and set them in the Verde River for this unit; the cheers that went out could be heard down the hall!

My third-grade classroom is composed of students who are from the Salt River Pima-Maricopa Indian Community. The Verde River is located on their reservation and provides an optimal outdoor classroom. This sacred and stunning piece of land is home to a rich bird, fish, and wild animal population, making it the perfect setting for our project.

The project was a large endeavor for students. First, they had to reach out to the Salt River tribe's Environmental Protection and Natural Resources department (SREPNR) to assist with this project. Students worked together to write a letter asking SREPNR for their support and to schedule a field trip to the river. The department responded immediately and favorably to the earnest student requests.

Later, several SREPNR scientists arrived at our classrooms and talked about the water quality of the Verde River and the different species that live in the riparian basin. This created an optimal learning environment that sparked the curiosity of the students who worked diligently planning their crayfish traps. As traps were being built, so was the question bank as they wanted to learn more about the river that sits in their own backyard.

Finally, the day arrived to set the crayfish traps! The entire third-grade learning community boarded a bus, and off to the river we went. Arriving at the river, the SREPNR scientists had tubs of bait for students to begin filling bait bags. This prep sparked all their senses: the fishy smell, the slimy touch, the curious sights. It was a new experience for them, and they let me know how excited they were by sharing what they were experiencing kinesthetically, verbally, and visually. When the students had their traps baited, they took the short hike to the river, where they met another scientist who helped them set the traps. Once this was done, students were set free to explore the area. They were curious about their river and spent a great deal of time in the gentle stream. As they waded in the water, conversations naturally emerged centering on how this natural resource could be protected for generations to come.

Some traps did not attract any crayfish, and others did. Students were discovering and using evidence they collected to construct explanations and develop arguments about novel ideas. This project was messy, stinky, dirty, and full of laughter. Every student was engaged. Gone were the labels we as educators assign students based on data, and in their place was simply learning through natural inquiry. Curiosity allowed them to gain ownership of their learning, organize their ideas, and use what they gained from this science project as a resource when recalling and reflecting. Just as the sun makes water shimmer, curiosity added a little sparkle to our learning standards.

CHAPTER 7

SPARKING CURIOSITY

YOU'LL NEVER LOOK AT A SUITCASE THE SAME WAY AFTER READING THIS!

Take a moment and think about two or three topics that you remember from your school learning experiences. Topics that made you curious, made you wonder, and made you intrinsically motivated to learn more. I have always preferred visual learning, and oftentimes, when my teachers would show movie clips, that visual experience allowed my curiosity to soar.

In third grade, we learned about the RMS *Titanic*, and I'll never forget the day we received our permission slip to watch the movie. "We need a permission slip? Oh, this must be good!" I thought. Over the course of a few days, we watched the two VHS tapes (yes, VHS), and I was hooked. I wanted my own Heart of the Ocean, I needed to have my own copy of the movie, and I craved every fact about shipwrecks and the real *Titanic*. My curiosity was piqued.

To this day, the *Titanic* is something that captivates me, and I even had the opportunity to go to Ireland in 2017 to visit the largest *Titanic* attraction in the world: Titanic Belfast. In many ways, I was taken back to my third-grade classroom as I explored the interactive videos, peered through the glass floor with a mock shipwreck below it, and boarded the SS *Nomadic,* the *Titanic*'s original tender ship. I tell you this story because that tiny learning gap I had in third grade was closed just by my teachers and me collectively exploring my curiosity. As teachers, recognizing that gap and exploring the various ways we can facilitate its closing is so beautifully powerful.

Shortly after my trip to Belfast, I began thinking of all the ways I could recreate that experience in my classroom.

In 2018, one of my students walked in on our second day of class, knowing how much I loved Harry Potter, and reached into his backpack for something. As he was doing so, he said, "Here, Ms. Lamb. I want you to have this." In his hand was a wand.

Knowing the sentimental value I place on objects in my own life, I couldn't very well take this wand from a student, so I told him, "Well, I can't take your wand. Which character does this wand belong to anyway?"

He said, "This is the wand that chose me at Universal, and I want you to have it." I intended to keep it for a brief time, but shortly after, he moved away. I still have it to this day, and it's what inspired me to begin doing a classroom activity that I call "What's in the Suitcase?"

When creating a unit launch activity, I try to think about what items best symbolize what we'll be learning and discussing, and then I try to find those items to put in the suitcase. For example, if we're going to be discussing justice, I might add a gavel. If we'll be discussing death, I'll put in a fake skull from the dollar store. When the students walk in, they see a slide with pictures of suitcases and the title "What's in the Suitcase?" I keep the suitcase closed and ask them to simply write down the numbers one through ten on their loose-leaf or scrap paper.

Then, as mysteriously as I can, I open the suitcase, similar to how my student opened his backpack and pulled out the wand, and begin to withdraw one item at a time. I say nothing as I hold each item up. The students' task is to write down what the item reminds them of and how they think it could relate to what we will be learning. At the end, they take turns discussing their different predictions and thoughts about each item. This same activity can be used again later as a review of how those items related to the unit, and perhaps, just maybe, they can add their own items to the suitcase, either literally or figuratively, that relate to what they learned.

If I could time-travel back to my third-grade self and do this activity with the *Titanic* unit, I can only imagine how easily I would fill that suitcase up with items, all because of a little curiosity and a lot of minding the gap.

THESE THREE BRAIN FACTS WILL CHANGE THE WAY YOU LESSON PLAN FOREVER

Earlier, we discussed how it is essential to have our students board the Wonder Train and mind the curiosity gap so that they are primed for learning. When we think about that priming process and our goals with sparking, cultivating, and co-creating curiosity, we must also consider the "when" and the "why" behind that.

In his book *How the Brain Learns*, David A. Sousa discusses when students are most likely to retain information during a learning episode (our lessons). Reflecting and building on the work of Madeline Hunter and Hermann Ebbinghaus, Sousa explains that we tend to remember the information from the beginning of a lesson first, the end of the lesson second, and the middle of the lesson last. He calls these periods "prime-time-1" (most retention), "prime-time-2" (second best), and "down-time" (least retention). In other words, students are more likely to remember what is presented first and last in a lesson than what is presented in the middle.

In a typical lesson, we might see the most important information we want to learn presented at the beginning of the lesson. Then, during that down-time, or the time in which there is the least amount of retention, we have them work and practice with the material and then apply it to further develop their long-term memory of it. During prime-time-2, our second-best time for retention, we close the lesson and have them make meaningful connections through reflections and exit tickets.

How does this relate to curiosity? Consider what you can do to prime your students for learning before they even walk in the door. This type of lesson preparation is often referred to as a lesson hook, anticipatory set, set induction, or advance organizer. According to presentational hook expert Dave Burgess, author of *Teach Like a Pirate*, the presentation hook is the sweet spot where content (your subject area), technique/method (your instructional strategies), and presentation (the presentational decisions you make to hook your students) coalesce. When we use these aspects to spark curiosity, you'll find the added benefit of improved memory and retention moving into prime-time-1 and as you close in prime-time-2.

This benefit is all thanks to the neurotransmitter dopamine. We already discussed the value of a dopamine blast in the earlier section on surprise, and curiosity is no different. Like the element of surprise, sparked curiosity creates a surge in dopamine, which triggers the brain's long-term memory region, the hippocampus. Therefore, sparking curiosity is an essential part of our teaching and learning process. In this section, you'll find our favorite ways to spark students' curiosity right before prime-time-1.

Look up

YOU'LL NEVER BELIEVE HOW EASY THESE CURIOSITY-SPARKING IDEAS ARE!

AMBIENT MEDIA

One of the simplest yet most effective curiosity-sparking tools requires no supplies and minimal effort. Taking one minute to search for ambient media on YouTube while sipping your morning coffee can yield a curiosity-sparking hook. The selection of ambient media is so diverse that it is easy to find a clip to fit your needs. Much like the ambient sounds mentioned in the Surprise section, ambient media combines sights and sounds that work wonders in piquing students' curiosity. Examples include presenting an animated field of flowers before a lesson on pollination, projecting a hip coffee shop during poetry reading, or playing an oceanfront setting after assigning an island-themed STEM challenge. Curious to see the vast selection of ambient media that's available? Search the first word that pops into your head plus "ambience" and see what appears!

RANDOM TRINKETS

Humans are curious creatures. If we notice something out of the norm or incongruous with our environment, then we have a natural inclination to check it out. Harness this tendency by placing random trinkets, such as props or signs, around your classroom leading up to a learning journey.

- A month before starting an anatomy unit, start placing plastic Halloween body parts in strange places around the classroom and feign confusion about how they got there.
- A week before starting *Animal Farm*, post the cryptic seven commandments around your classroom without explaining their purpose.

- A day before beginning a web design unit, stick a range of professional web designer fees on each device and have students wonder what the numbers might mean.
- An hour before teaching a history unit, decorate your door with images of diverse and important figures, and then have students tell you how many of these history-makers they immediately recognize as they walk into your classroom.
- A minute before teaching a new math concept, post a collage of things that wouldn't exist without this concept and have students wonder about the connection as they learn.

When you pique students' curiosity through novel items in their environment, they will be more interested in closing their information gap to find out what the trinkets might mean.

GALLERY WALKS

Don't destroy that gap! At the beginning of a new unit, it may be tempting to lecture, assign reading, or otherwise "fill the gap" for students to prepare them for the learning experience ahead. Instead of jumping right into your role as tour guide, give your students a chance to wonder and explore a topic on their own first. You can do this by curating artifacts, transforming your classroom into a mini-museum, and hosting a gallery walk for your students.

The artifacts can be nearly anything: images, questions, excerpts, primary sources, quotes, mentor texts, multimedia, etc. If students can observe it, contemplate it, question it, and discuss it, then grab some tape and put it on display in your gallery. Then, ask students to circulate around the room and respond in some way. The response component can be as open-ended or as structured as you'd like. Students can respond to each piece via specific questions or a simple graphic organizer, they can use sticky notes to add their thoughts to the artifacts, or they can discuss with their peers as they circulate and synthesize their findings at the end.

You can even add intrigue by enforcing a "silent discussion" gallery walk, where students contribute their thoughts only in writing. Whatever way you structure it, this inquiry-based approach is sure to spark students' curiosity because it commands them to generate questions and conclusions based on the limited amount of information they have. After all, that is precisely what we want: a chance to delay information just long enough to create a gap and a thirst for learning.

LEARNING STATIONS

Before embarking on a long learning journey, give students a little taste of the trip with stations designed to unleash their natural curiosity. First, pose an essential question; it could be "What were the Roaring Twenties like?" or "What is the definition of modernism?" Then, create a set of learning stations that will encourage students to discover meaning and answer the question on their own. The more challenging the question and elusive the answer, the better. Allow students to question the content, wrestle with it, test it, and guess about it. Let them struggle a little bit—it's good for them, and over time this kind of lesson will become less of a frustrating chore and more of a challenge in curiosity.

When you bring students back together after the learning stations, you will have a living, collective answer, one that transcends any textbook definition or explanation that you might have given your students in the first place. And even better than answers, you'll most likely have a new set of curious questions that can inform your upcoming instruction. You'll close one gap, but create a few more, continuing the endless dance of curiosity.

PERSONALITY QUIZZES

Another way to tease students with just enough information to incite curiosity is through magazine-style personality "quizzes" that relate to the upcoming content. For inspiration, head to the grocery store checkout line tabloids or do a quick search on BuzzFeed. While we are a little skeptical of BuzzFeed's logic in some quizzes (e.g., "Which piece of IKEA furniture are you?"), we can't deny that these fun quizzes have stolen a few minutes of our time.

Spoiler alert: Most of these quizzes have little educational value, but that doesn't mean we can't create spin-off versions for our teaching content. While they do require some extra creativity and a dose of ridiculousness, when done right, you absolutely can use them to trick your students into getting curious for the unit ahead. For example, Abby loves to give her students a "How Transcendental Are You?" quiz as a way to spark a discussion about the tenets of transcendentalism before reading the texts of Emerson and Thoreau. Ashley does the same before teaching romanticism, giving her students a pop quiz titled "Romantic or Realist?"

When you create these quizzes, make sure that there is some sort of points system for the answer choices (one point for every yes, or a 4-3-2-1 point system for A-B-C-D answer choices) so that students can decipher what the answers reveal about the unit. After "assigning" the quiz and laughing at students' initial groans, ask them to reflect on the quiz, list as much as they can gather about the new content, or write a definition for the topic. Then, facilitate a discussion and allow students to share how they curiously "thought backward" to draw conclusions from their quiz answers.

To get you thinking, here are some other fun ideas:

- Science: What type of matter are you?
- Social Studies: What type of government are you?
- Art: Which art period are you?
- Math: Which equation are you?

If you're curious enough, take our quiz below to see an example of exactly what we mean!

WHAT TYPE OF SCHOOL SUPPLY ARE YOU?

Answer the prompts below to find out what type of school supply you are.

1) In staff meetings you tend to . . .
   a) show off your new planner.
   b) challenge your principal.
   c) think about your students.
   d) take diligent notes.

2) Your lesson style is . . .
   a) all about variety. You love changing it up every day.
   b) big and bold. You're loud and confident.
   c) reflective and student-centered. You focus on the kids.
   d) standards-focused. You found what works, and you stick to it.

3) Your classroom management style is . . .
   a) an ultra-organized system. Having a detailed behavior chart and procedure list fixes everything.
   b) all about you. You make the rules, and your students fall in line.
   c) democratic. You decide on the expectations as a class.
   d) dictated by your principal. You memorized the school handbook to a T.

4) You eat lunch with . . .
   a) different people every day. Sometimes you eat in the teachers' lounge; other times, you meet up with your co-teacher. It changes day to day.

    b) your friends in the teachers' lounge. You're the life of the party.

    c) your students. It's important to spend this time with them. *I walk home*

    d) yourself. ~~You prefer to avoid any potential problems~~.

5) Your classroom decor is . . .

    a) eclectic. You like to mix and match all of your favorite things and colors.

    b) bold. You choose bold colors and in-your-face posters.

    c) student-made. All of your decor was created by students.

    d) school-issued. You display school-sponsored information.

6) When you grade work, you . . .

    a) often misplace it.

    b) love writing feedback and giving stickers.

    c) conference with students.

    d) use the school-issued rubric.

If you answered mostly A's, you're a **Flair pen** teacher! You've got style every day (not just on picture day)! You love bright, flashy lessons, and you have a variety of strategies to back them up. Your color-coded planner looks pretty, but you're often scattered. You tend to overextend your grip on all of your colorful passions, but you're able to adjust when you miss the mark.

If you answered mostly B's, you're a **microphone** teacher! You like big, bold declarations, and you're not afraid to ruffle a few feathers. You're loud and proud, a born entertainer. For you, teaching is a song and dance, literally. Sometimes you can be a little overpowering, but you've learned to tone it down when necessary.

If you answered mostly C's, you're a **glue stick** teacher. You're dependable and trustworthy. Every student and coworker comes to you because they know you'll patch up their problems. For you, teaching is all about forming close bonds with your students. You might not be loud and flashy, but you always stick to a task to see it through, and your relationship with your students is permanent.

If you answered mostly D's, you're a **ruler** teacher. You're all about the straight and narrow. You follow the rules and you expect your students to do the same. You can be a little too rigidly hyperfocused on your path, but everyone respects your constancy, dedication, and poise.

INFERENCE CHALLENGE

A little bit of a challenge goes a long way when it comes to stimulating students' curiosity. Before starting a new unit or beginning a new novel, try supplying students with just enough information to create an incentivizing knowledge gap. Then, pose the inference challenge, an engaging spin-off of the classic KWL (know, want to know, learn) chart, and ask students to list as many inferences or predictions as possible from the clues given. Encourage them to make as many educated guesses as they can, give them the chance to share their conclusions with their peers, and then facilitate a whole-class discussion to further hook them before beginning the unit.

This approach works particularly well before reading a book in ELA classes, especially a text with a film version. Because movie trailers highlight dramatic scenes, employ compelling snippets of dialogue, offer a glimpse into characterization, and strategically create anticipation, they are the perfect "text" to closely read. Except it won't *feel* like close reading, but rather an investigative inference challenge. This activity will spark students' curiosity, create questions in their mind, stimulate predictions, and inevitably lead to more active, engaged reading. If a movie trailer isn't available, try finding intriguing passages from the text and then asking students to investigate them for inferences about the characters and plot before reading.

FIRST CHAPTER FRIDAY

Capitalize on the brain's inherent love for storytelling and create the ultimate curiosity gap with First Chapter Friday. This low-prep and high-impact activity is exactly what it sounds like: every Friday, read aloud the first chapter of a new book. The more conflict, unanswered questions, and cliffhangers, the merrier! Give students a tantalizing taste of a book, just enough to hook them into reading. Over time, you will learn more about your readers' preferences and learn how to recommend the right books to pique their curiosity.

In addition to cultivating a classroom full of curious readers, First Chapter Friday will expose your students to more books than your curriculum could on its own. By featuring a different book every Friday, you will be able to highlight thirty-six books, stories, authors, and perspectives over the course of the year. As you search for books to share, it is critical to select an inclusive range of titles that represent both your students' perspectives *and* experiences different from their own. We recommend checking out book lists from Project LIT Community (@projectlitcomm on Instagram), the #ownvoices hashtag on Twitter, the 28 Days Later initiative from the Brown Bookshelf, and resources on the We Need Diverse Books website.

BOOK TRAILER TUESDAY

What's even easier than turning the page? Pressing play! Similar to First Chapter Friday, Book Trailer Tuesday is all about hooking students on books by bringing them to life on the big screen. Thanks to the variety of quick book trailers available on YouTube, this feat

Book Sites

create a book trailer

can be accomplished in less than five minutes a week. Warning: If you try this, you'll be surprised at how incredibly easy it is. Just sit back, relax, and press play. Then, give students a chance to share their thoughts, questions, and reactions while you remind them that they'll "have to read to find out!"

If you love the idea of First Chapter Friday but don't have the time or energy to commit to it, Book Trailer Tuesday is an engaging, easier alternative. And if you're already on the first chapter train, then book trailers will complement that perfectly. By implementing both Book Trailer Tuesday and First Chapter Friday, you will be able to highlight seventy-two different books! With those odds, you can guarantee that pages will turn and curiosity sparks will fly.

Many texts do not have book trailers, so if there is a title you want to feature, feel free to get creative and utilize other resources. For example, there is currently no official book trailer for Elizabeth Acevedo's *The Poet X*, but there are other videos with interviews and author fun facts that would work well as a teaser for the text.

Book Trailer Tuesday

*⌢Abby

When I began Book Trailer Tuesday and First Chapter Friday, my goal was to feature a wide, inclusive range of books to supplement a curriculum that was lacking diverse texts. After starting out the year strong, I decided to feature "spooky" books during the month of October. New to the world of seventh grade and still learning about middle school texts, I relied on book recommendations, bestseller lists, and "top ten" style articles to find a fun collection of scary stories to share with my students. Halfway through the month, I looked back on the titles I had featured. All of them had been written by white authors. Disappointed in myself and the disservice I had done to my students, I reflected, and then quickly got to work.

In my rush to find books that fit what I thought was a fun theme, I had slid back into the system of whiteness and racism that I was attempting to resist in the first place. This was a powerful reminder that the default is white: the search engines, the bestsellers, and the articles all pointed me to the so-called creepy "classics." I had reverted to this default because I was in a rush and unfamiliar with a new grade level. But these were *not* excuses, and the only thing scary about my book choices was this negligence. I knew that as an educator, it was my responsibility to take the extra step, run more searches, and seek out better resources. If I had time to plan and facilitate activities like First Chapter Friday, then I had time to find better books that didn't center whiteness.

While I did go on to find incredible books by authors of color and feature them for our following Book Trailer Tuesdays and First Chapter Fridays, I reminded myself that no whimsical theme or activity is more important than antiracism. And if I can't find an inclusive book, then I'm not searching hard enough.

Now, when I am searching for a certain genre, theme, or topic, I add more specific terms to my searches. Googling "best middle grade fantasy books" is not enough; if I want texts written by Black authors, I have to include that. I have to specify if I want books featuring Indigenous perspectives, "own voices" titles, or texts featuring an inclusive cast of characters. In addition to specific searches, I keep a spreadsheet to track the books I share and reflect on opportunities for representation.

Every book I include, as well as any story I exclude, sends a message to my students. I want that message to be *you matter,* and I want those stories to serve as mirrors, windows, and sliding glass doors to their rich, complex, and unique lives.

EXPERIMENTS

Replicating experiments and incorporating the results at the start of a learning journey not only sparks curiosity about the experiment itself, but also presents a built-in learning gap in which students remain engaged until the purpose of the experiment is revealed.

Clean Hands, Clean Minds: Before reading the "Out, damned spot!" scene in *Macbeth*, Ashley has her students replicate the hand-washing experiment outlined in the article "Clean Hands, Clean Minds: The Psychological Impact of Physical Cleanliness" from *Big Think* by Maria Konnikova. Half the class is given a list of immoral actions to read, such as "bullying someone online," and the other half is given moral actions to read, like "volunteering at the humane society." Next, both groups are given the exact same fill-in-the-letter words, such as W_ _H and S_ _P. As the original and official study concludes, students who read the immoral actions are more likely to fill in the letters to make "clean words" such as WASH and SOAP. Those who read the moral list are more likely to fill in the words randomly with words like WISH and STOP. Students' curiosity is sparked by the experiment itself, then prolonged as they must read Shakespeare's scene to find the connection and close the information gap for the implications of the experiment.

Negativity bias: To spark curiosity during a high school journalism unit on newsworthiness and facilitate a discussion over "negativity bias" in the news, Abby conducts a social experiment under the guise of a typical "Article of the Day" assignment. Instead of giving students one article to read, she gives them a choice of two articles via a Google form: one, a heartwarming story about an animal who saved the day, and another, a report chronicling a recent murder. Students select an article, read it, and respond to it with no idea that their teacher is using this to answer her own curious questions: *Will her students uphold what psychologists have long found to be true? Are humans inherently attracted to negative news?* Time after time, her students overwhelmingly read the negative article, even though many of them adamantly assert that they "like good news" and "the news is too negative." After revealing the purpose of the mini social experiment to her guinea pigs—or students—Abby facilitates a compelling whole-class discussion as students try to wrap their mind around this disconnect between what they *think* they prefer and what they actually want to read. This simple twist on the content always creates more questions in students' minds, inquiries that Abby then uses to make the rest of the unit a richer, memorable learning experience.

Gender stereotyping: In order to facilitate a social experiment before analyzing gender stereotypes, Jenna asks her students to take out a piece of paper and fold it in fours. Their curiosity is sparked with this unusual request. Then, without revealing the experiment, she asks them to draw four pictures: a kindergarten teacher, a lawyer, a doctor, and a nurse, with identifying characteristics like clothes, hair, and accessories. Once they're finished, she reveals that the intent of the social experiment is to explore societal gender stereotypes for professions. Generally, they discover that the majority of students draw the lawyer and doctor as men and the kindergarten teacher and nurse as women. Sometimes, they discover that students who had different representations generally have personal experiences with individuals who break gender stereotypes. Because the results of this experiment are unpredictable, there is always something new to learn, and students' interest in this lens of analysis is piqued in new ways.

The bystander effect: Staci loves a good social experiment, and she explores the bystander effect in a variety of her texts and units relating to individuality, conformity, responsibility, etc. Consider trying out a simple experiment in your classroom: Pretend to lose something sentimental to you. Prior to class, clue at least one student in on the experiment, so that when you announce you're looking for the item, at least that one student will offer to help find it. You'll probably notice that once one or two students start to help find this item, more students will get involved. It's a domino effect of participation. Staci also uses clips from the show *What Would You Do?* On the show, they stage scenarios in social settings to see how people react. Some people choose to intervene and aid someone in a distressed situation, and some people choose to ignore the situation and not get involved. More often than not, what we see is that people are more likely to act a certain way or intervene if others do so first. Similarly, people are more likely to avoid a situation if they see other people avoiding it. After trying out these ideas, continue reflecting on and exploring these ideas as social situations come up in your curriculum.

THE FIRST SLIDE

As we reflect on sparking curiosity, we want you to remember that doing so doesn't have to be a time-consuming, labor-intensive activity. Maybe you have little time after school to decorate and transform your room. Maybe you have five preps and find it challenging to implement a variety of instructional activities. Maybe you have little autonomy in your curriculum and aren't sure how to navigate curiosity in your own way. Whatever challenges you may come across, we want you to remember this: the Power of the First Slide. It might seem silly capitalizing it in such a way, but our students are naturally drawn to look at wherever you typically present your agenda. We like to know what's going to happen. It's human nature, and you have an opportunity every day to hook your students with just one slide.

For example, Staci has a slide with images of books, cookies, and popcorn that she uses for book tastings, an activity that allows students to get a "taste" of a book before they completely commit to it. Throughout the year, she usually includes four or five book tastings, and every time her students see that slide, they know what's coming: cookies and popcorn (with an entrée of reading and analysis, of course!). That one slide changes the mood, heightens their anticipation, and sparks them just enough to question, "What are we starting today? What are we reading?"

Another way to use the Power of the First Slide is to project images and current events that students know. When students are knowledgeable on a topic, they love to let everyone know. Staci saw this firsthand with her nonfiction unit, in which they read *Just Mercy*. First, she showed the trailer for the TV series *When They See Us*, so on the first slide that day, she projected a marketing image from Netflix. When the students who knew the content walked in, she was met with "This was so good! Are we watching this?" and "Yes! Yes! Yes!"

What happens with first slides like this is students' excitement and knowledge then create a wave of contagious curiosity. People like being excited to know more, and when students see their peers excited, they want to know what excites them about it. When you can, use that prime-time-1 gap and have something on your screen that will do just enough to prep them for the learning and content that is about to take place. One simple slide can do that.

Staci

I first learned about David Sousa's work in one of my graduate classes, and since then, I often keep prime-time-1 and prime-time-2 in mind as I lesson plan. One simple way to capitalize on this is to use trendy content hooks.

In 2019, an adorable, pint-sized, 50-year-old "baby" took the world by surprise, curiosity, and memes. Lots of memes. I'll be the first to admit that my obsession with Baby Yoda, now formally known as Grogu, began with the memes, and after I watched *The Mandalorian* in 2020, I fell in love even more.

My students could see my obsession from the random merchandise I would wear/have, and then I started to incorporate my own memes into my slides as a way to add some humor to our lessons.

One day, I decided to have Grogu become my co-teacher to help me teach dialogue as part of our narrative unit. While I was adorned with my Grogu T-shirt and my Grogu hat, he was with us around the classroom in the forms of adorable pictures, memes, and check-ins throughout every activity and slide we did and saw that day. From the beginning of that lesson, my goal was to pique my students' curiosity with some trendy content, and from there, they were engaged and primed to learn.

At the start of the lesson, in prime-time-1, I explicitly taught the rules of dialogue and provided examples of correctly punctuated dialogue. As we proceeded into down-time, students had the opportunity to practice by writing dialogue for meme-like pictures I gave them, and the results were hilarious. During prime-time-2, for closure, I had students reflect on the narratives they were writing and consider where and how they could embed dialogue into their own writing. During prime-time-2, we want students to find meaning and value in the work, and connecting it to their own writing helped them apply what they had learned in prime-time-1.

I'd like to take credit for the success of the overall lesson, but I know my fabulous co-teacher had a lot to do with it, especially his help during prime-time-1.

★ ★ ★

While these initial curiosity sparks may be diverse in nature, piquing students' curiosity can help them better reach an epistemic level of learning. According to educational researcher Mary Helen Immordino-Yang, "Curiosity can predict not only how much teens will remember about a story they've read, but also how thoughtfully they reflect on the story's characters." Therefore, tapping into students' curiosity at the start of a learning journey can send them down an epistemic track of deeper reflection and analysis.

Although neuroscience still has a long way to go to fully understand how curiosity impacts the brain, one thing is clear: curiosity is a catalyst for learning. Once we can spark students' curiosity, the fire of their own intrinsic motivation will take them even further than we could have. We like to think that this is what Einstein meant when he said, "I never teach my pupils. I only attempt to provide the conditions in which they can learn." We have the power to provide conditions that fuel curiosity. As you now know, all it takes is one single spark.

CHAPTER 8

CULTIVATING CURIOSITY

HOW YOU COULD BE ROBBING STUDENTS OF THE WORLD WITHOUT EVEN KNOWING IT

There's an Iroquois creation story in which a woman of the Sky World became curious about the bark that covered the roots of the Great Tree. This tree was not like any other tree. It was tremendous, sacred, inspiring, and revered. Its massive roots grew beyond the Sky World and its fruitful branches expanded above it. The woman's interest in the bark of the roots became so obsessive that she convinced her husband to dig a hole in the floor of the Sky World so that she could better reach the roots. When the husband completed the task, he became so fearful of what he saw below that he cowered. But that which made the husband fearful made the wife bold. Her head filled with curiosity, she bent over the hole, looked down at the ocean far below, and leaned so far into her wonder that she toppled out of the Sky World and fell into the unknown. This curiosity-spurred journey changed everything.

Through creation stories, cautionary tales, caring parents, and controlling educators, we are often taught to fear curiosity and its consequences. However, the very lessons that are meant to tame our inquisitiveness may also be hindering our advancement. As research has shown, cultivating, rather than condemning, curiosity is essential for deep understanding.

We've all had the experience of being right in the middle of making an epic point when a student eagerly raises his hand. You call on him in excited anticipation hoping he will endorse the knowledge bomb you are currently dropping, but alas, the pressing question out of his mouth is "Can I go to the bathroom?"

Likewise, most educators have also experienced engaging students in a topic, such as the author's choice of setting, when an inquisitive student blurts out, "Do you think deserted islands are real? If you found one, could you just claim it as your own? How would you get drinking water? How fast would salt water kill you?"

Though these common classroom occurrences differ in questioning level, both scenarios disrupt the flow of class and can become annoying at times. However, it's how you respond to the off-topic yet inquisitive questioning that models the importance you place on cultivating curiosity within your classroom.

Instead of condemning curiosity with . . .	Consider cultivating curiosity with . . .
Please don't interrupt.	I love that you are curious about that, so let's write down our questions now and come back to them in just a moment.
That's not relevant right now.	Thank you for that question; let's explore it after we finish this task!
I don't know.	I don't have the answer for that, but now I'm curious!
What did you learn?	What are you curious about right now?
Do you have any questions?	What questions do you have?

When we encourage students' curiosity, we condition them to question more, probe more, engage more, and learn more. When the Iroquois woman fell into the unknown, she did not perish. Instead, she interacted with her new surroundings on a turtle's back, leaned into her curiosities, and created a whole new world to explore—Earth. Having an educator who cultivates curiosity rather than condemns it could open up a whole new educational world for students. Curiosity is the engine behind a "have to learn" and a "want to learn" mindset.

Now, we turn to Derrick Carlson, an elementary teacher in Chicago, to illuminate the "want to learn" mindset. Notice how Derrick's dialogue cultivates curiosity rather than condemns it.

WONDER MAKER

DERRICK CARLSON (⌾ @BLACKANDBRIGHTIN2ND)

ARE YOU MORE OBSERVANT THAN A SECOND GRADER?

"This is going to be the easiest part of the first six weeks," I think to myself. I am walking down to the printer and I am excited to get going with our geography unit. Plate tectonics is usually a hit for my students; they love learning about volcanoes and earthquakes and how it all happens. I am excited to connect this unit to traveling, planetary geology, and other topics I can interconnect and help the students begin to contextualize the information as we embed skill building inside the unit.

After I get everything printed out, I walk over to pick up my class from their specials class. A student in line asks, "Why do you look so happy?" I smile and say, "I think you will love the lesson today!"

As we move back to the classroom, everyone takes their seat at the rug, and they have such a look of anticipation for the lesson to start! I introduce the class to the geography unit and pose our essential question, "How do geography and land impact how folx live and behave?"

I begin by playing a quick clip that shows an eruption. They stare at the screen and watch the twenty-second clip. We begin to discuss how the volcano was created and how folx who live near the volcano might behave or live differently to prepare in case the volcano erupts. I ask, "What would they need to do and what would they need to adjust in order to prepare for a volcanic eruption?" I take a few responses, write them on our T-chart, and pose this question to the students: "Now that we have discussed how land and volcanoes are an important part of the lives of the folx who live near them, what are ways that we have to adjust our behavior and lifestyle for where we live?"

To prepare them for discussion, we do some vocabulary and background knowledge-building. After we discuss terminology for the land features and the geologic formation, I ask students to describe the area in which we live: "We live in the Midwest and it is very flat. How does this impact our lifestyle and how folx act?" Students then turn to a partner to discuss, but after leaning in to listen to their partner talk, I come to the realization that they are not really sure what they've noticed about their own geography! I recognize that I not only have to teach them about geography concepts, but also how to be curious about patterns of behavior they notice in their own lives, and how they relate to the land and features around us.

Pivoting, we name the features of our regional area. I show students a few different maps related to population and land-forms to build background knowledge and spark their curiosity about where folx live based upon income, gender, and race. A student raises her hand and asks, "Why do some folx only live by the lake while others are far away?"

Finally, I shift my approach for the rest of the lesson. I tell the students, "I notice with our area that we might not have some of the same geologic features as other areas we study, but I know there are some really interesting things here in the Great Lakes region." We begin discussing this, and I tell them, "We have to think about the world we live in, rather than just exist. We have to ask ourselves why groups of folx behave in certain ways and live in certain areas." The focus of the lesson is no longer about learning the features and definitions; it is about teaching students to be curious about their own lives. I need to get students thinking about how social constructs intersect with geography.

This lesson I described was organic, and the students started coming to school asking a lot of questions and sharing their observations from the community. They became interested in the conversations about housing and where folx live in relation to the water. They learned through their curiosity about housing discrimination and wealth distribution. I was glad they became part of this inquiry process, because it carried them into the year with authentic and relevant engagement. So, while my unit did not end up nearly as easy as I'd imagined, it actually provided a much deeper level of reflection in the long run. Cultivating my second graders' curiosity about their local geography ignited a lifelong learning skill in observing the world around them.

HAVE YOU EVER BEEN SO CURIOUS ABOUT SOMETHING THAT YOU WOULD PAY FOR AN ANSWER?

In "The Wick in the Candle of Learning: Epistemic Curiosity Activates Reward Circuitry and Enhances Memory," researchers studied participants reading trivia questions and tracked their curiosity as it correlated with their confidence on the answers. When trivia players were either completely confused about the answer or overly confident, they were not very curious. However, when they were somewhat confident but not totally sure of the answer, their curiosity was at its peak. In fact, some participants were so curious that they reported they would even pay to know the trivia answers. Furthermore, the more curious the participants were, the more likely they were to remember the trivia answers one to two weeks later.

While we don't think our students will ever volunteer to pay us out of sheer curiosity, we are encouraged by this concept of a "sweet spot" for curiosity because it's something that we can learn to cultivate in our classrooms. Surely, we can dangle *just enough information* in front of our students and watch them become captivated with a thirst for more.

A study in the neuroscience journal *Neuron* demonstrated similar effects: higher-curiosity trivia questions resulted in better recall of answers. But this time, researchers threw in a seemingly random twist to test another question: Would highly curious participants recall "incidental material"? In between the questions and answers, researchers flashed a random human face on the screen. As it turned out, heightened curiosity resulted in increased recall of the faces, even though they were entirely irrelevant to the trivia. In other words, if you can manage to pique your students' curiosity at the beginning of a lesson (even one that might be dry and boring), you will have primed the pump for learning.

HOW TO CULTIVATE CURIOSITY IN JUST TWO MINUTES

While learning reflections are an effective way to facilitate much-needed metacognition, they also offer a chance to promote curiosity. The next time you ask students to reflect on their learning, include the following questions:

- What was the most interesting or intriguing thing you learned?
- What do you want to learn more about?
- What questions do you have?

This progression of questions guides students toward curiosity. It's easy for them to note something interesting that they learned, a little more demanding to identify what they don't know but want to learn, and most challenging to generate their own questions on the topic. The more you facilitate learning reflections, the more natural this process will become for students. Learning reflections don't need to be time-consuming, formal, or graded assignments. Consider incorporating a quick two-minute reflection exit ticket at the end of every lesson or week. Investing a few minutes in this exercise will help your students flex their curiosity muscles every day, and before you know it, they will be reflecting, questioning, and contemplating on their own.

THE ONE QUESTION THAT CHANGES EVERYTHING

Cultivating curiosity is as simple as asking students to be more observant of the world around them. The next time you want to show them some kind of example, mentor text, phenomenon, primary source, or problem, resist the temptation of explaining it to them. Even resist the temptation of asking specific, analytical questions. Don't lecture. Don't lead. Instead, simply pose this powerful question: *What do you notice?*

Odds are, you will be pleasantly surprised with just how much students notice when you give them the chance, endure that initial awkward silence, and encourage their observations. The first time you introduce this activity, students may struggle, but after some modeling and repeated practice, they will become skilled observers. You can even add in some healthy competition by telling them, "First period noticed twenty different things! Can you top that?" to encourage them to look for the little things they otherwise wouldn't notice. As ELA teachers, we are all about noticing, questioning, and reading between the lines. Here are a few of our favorite ways to weave in the powerful "What do you notice?" question:

> **Mentor texts:** If you're struggling to incorporate mentor texts in your classroom, simplify your approach with the "What

do you notice?" technique. The next time you introduce a genre of writing, don't start with a mini-lesson. Instead, find various examples of the genre and give students the time to comb through the professional examples and catalog everything they notice. If the question is too broad, consider scaffolding it with more specific questions: "What do you notice about the structure?" "What do you notice about the word choice?" "What do you notice about the punctuation?" The list goes on!

Close reading: The elusive concept of "close reading" can be challenging for students, so try structuring it with a simple "What do you notice?" approach. For example, after the first "round" of close reading, ask students: "What do you notice about what the author is saying?" (comprehension). For the second read-through, challenge them to think a little deeper: "What do you notice about how the author is saying it?" (author's craft). And for the final reading, pose this question: "What do you notice about why the author is saying it?" (author's purpose).

Analyzing art: The Weisman Art Museum created a strategy called PERCEIVE, a process that leads viewers through perception and speculation of visual art images, but the strategy can be used with other media and texts as well. Can you guess what question they ask first? That's right! "What do you notice?" In a powerful audio recording on their website of this process in action, a student, Alston Riley, is guided by his teacher, Melissa Borgmann. Together, they work through the PERCEIVE questions about one of Douglas Argue's paintings, formally called *Untitled*, but referred to by many as the "Chicken Painting." Alston's personality is amazingly contagious, and in just under four minutes, his analysis and curiosity about a painting of a bunch of chickens are beautifully captured.

Here are a few ways to adapt the "What do you notice?" activity for different content areas:

- **Social studies:** Provide students with a primary source, such as a political cartoon or the front page of a newspaper (NewseumED is a great source for this).
- **Science:** Allow students to observe a reaction, phenomenon, or experiment, and ask them to catalog every detail that they notice through the process.
- **Math:** Give students a complex word problem, but before they solve it, ask them to brainstorm a bullet-point list of everything they notice.
- **Physical education:** When teaching a new exercise or physical activity, model it first and ask students to note the form, rules, and benefits.

Another variation of this activity involves giving students various examples—the good, the bad, and the ugly—without telling them which version is the best example. Students can list what they notice about each example, discuss their observations with peers, and then "grade" or rate the examples. They can even note what questions they would ask the creators of each example, depending on the assignment. Once students have noted what they noticed, discussed their conclusions, generated questions, and evaluated the examples, you can facilitate a much more powerful whole-class discussion.

The classic "What do you notice?" activity is the perfect way to train your students to become more curious, but it also doubles as a way to generate the informal data you need to plan your subsequent lessons. Once you see what your students notice, you will learn what they don't know, and you can adjust your instruction to mind this gap.

THE #1 THING WE LOVE BUT HATE TO ADMIT

Humans naturally crave conflict and controversy. We are curious—often morbidly so—about violence, crime, controversy, death, and despair. It's why bad news dominates the headlines and true crime podcasts top the charts. Whether we'd like to admit it or not, we are fascinated with conflict. This, too, may stem from a gap. While psychologists have differing theories to explain our predilection for negative news, one is that we tend to have an idealistic view of the world. Because of the gap between our perspective and reality, we are all the more shocked and drawn to the negative.

To be clear, you certainly don't need to change your curriculum to reflect everything that's wrong with the world. But if you want to use this curious attraction to conflict to your advantage, then a healthy dose of controversy can go a long way in creating extra engagement. Here are a few ideas for creating the kind of friction that will foster curiosity:

> **Class polls:** Pose a controversial question related to your content, and then facilitate a quick class poll to spark some curious discussion. Consider using a digital platform like Google Forms or Poll Everywhere to show students live results. Better yet, encourage your students to conduct their own polls and surveys when they catch the curiosity bug!
>
> **Debates:** Create conflict and stimulate curious, critical thinking by incorporating more opportunities for debate. Whether you facilitate impromptu debates, speed debates (more on those later), Lincoln-Douglas debates, or whole-class debates, you will be sure to engage your learners in a more dynamic way.
>
> **Structured academic controversies:** A balanced twist to traditional debates, a structured academic controversy asks students to collaborate and synthesize in order to come to a consensus. Developed by David W. Johnson and Roger T.

Johnson, a structured controversy begins with a debatable question and groups of four students composed of two-person teams. After reading provided documents and sources, each team is responsible for defending a position. However, when the two-person teams come together as four, the goal transcends debate. First, the teams must present their defense with the goal of teaching the other side, not "winning" the argument. Finally, after listening to the opposing viewpoints, the group of four must work together to reach a consensus on the issue.

As you can see, cultivating curiosity is about embracing the unknown and taking a turn down a new road, just for the thrill of exploring it. It's an adventure with no itinerary other than the wondering and wandering, a chance to finally follow the compelling questions of *Why? What if?* and *What do you notice?*

The more you allow your students to indulge in these questions, the more curious they will become. That's why we love curiosity: it's the gift that keeps on giving.

Maggie — on trial
- *Pete*
- *Mom*
- *Jimmy*
- *Neighbors*

audio? version.

CHAPTER 9

CO-CREATING CURIOSITY

ONLY A TRUE TEACHER CAN RELATE TO THIS METAPHOR

*Jenna

The journey that we're on to create classrooms full of wonder can be both exciting and daunting, just like when we prepare for travel in our personal lives. On one hand, I am an adventurer at heart ready to see the world. On the other hand, I am a multitasking machine, checking and rechecking my itinerary and to-do list. Take our trip to Salem, Massachusetts, for our live Keeping the Wonder Workshop in the fall of 2019 as an example.

We had more than one hundred educators coalescing in historic Salem, Massachusetts, for a day of magical learning at the gothic Hammond Castle in Gloucester. Naturally, we had a long (and ever-expanding) to-do list of pre-workshop prep. Still, we were determined to spend a few personal hours exploring Salem.

Many of us (myself included) were about to experience Salem for the first time. There was so much to do, but little time to do it. A quick Google search yielded a fascinating result: a guided walking tour of Salem called Bewitched After Dark. The tagline teased, "Where the history is more frightening than fiction." We booked immediately. For a group of teachers, this was the perfect combination of history, expertise, and intrigue.

And our tour guide, Sarah, delivered.

We marveled at her impressive knowledge of Salem history, we snapped pictures of historical markers and memorials, and we brainstormed ways to bring this allure back to our classrooms in just under two bewitching hours. Our intrinsic curiosity may have brought us to Salem, but our tour guide nurtured that curiosity into something much more profound. I was particularly moved by the famous Salem Witch Trials Memorial, so I started doing some individual research in preparation to teach *The Crucible*. I dove deeper into the social and political controversy surrounding the memorial (the reason it took three hundred years for it to be built). Not only did this discovery provide a new lens to analyze *The Crucible*, but it also led us to create our own memorial in my classroom.

★ ★ ★

What we learned from this experience is that curiosity is co-created— and that sometimes it requires a guide. Have you caught on to the metaphor we're working with in this section? Congratulations! You're a true teacher!

HOW TO GROW A FOLLOWING OF CURIOUS SUPERFANS

When guests arrive at a tour destination, they are already curious. They booked the tour because of that curiosity, after all. Therefore, the role of the tour guide is to make it easier for them to focus and develop the curiosity they already have. So goes the role share of the teacher.

All children have curiosity. It's inherent. But our students just might not know how to channel that curiosity. That's where we come in. Fortunately, it can be as effortless as a friendly smile, according to researchers Susan Engel and Hilary Hackmann. In a fascinating study about student curiosity, they found that the more a teacher smiled and offered encouraging support, the more curious students were toward a "curious box" that had been strategically planted in the room.

Similarly, in an MIT study titled "Can Children Catch Curiosity from a Social Robot?" researchers found that even curious "social robots" could stimulate curiosity in young children by demonstrating enthusiasm for learning, wondering out loud, and asking targeted questions. Researchers concluded that "manipulating subtle social interaction utterances and expressions can impact children's curiosity." This research demonstrates that the teacher-as-tour-guide model really just means that "the curiosity classroom is co-created," as curiosity expert Wendy Ostroff writes in her book, *Cultivating Curiosity in K–12 Classrooms*. A tour guide teacher can ignite students' stagnant curiosity by engaging them with their own curiosity.

The "Sage of the Stage" model must give way to the "Guide on the Side" model in order to facilitate curiosity. We are certainly not advocating for a free-for-all classroom management style. On the contrary, we're advocating for lessons and activities with thoughtful structure and intention built in to (1) provide student-centered learning opportunities and (2) highlight and celebrate student voices.

To define the characteristics of a successful tour guide, we'll defer to one of the most famous tour guides in the world, Rick Steves. Hailed as "America's most respected authority on European travel," Steves is a travel writer, public television show host, blogger, and of course, tour guide. He even has a dedicated following of superfans that call themselves "Rickniks." It's easy to see why. With a quick perusal of his website, you'll find some key elements that we think lead to his success as a tour guide and explain his thousands of glowing reviews:

- **Passion:** A good tour guide is passionate about their content and teaching others.
- **Inclusivity:** A good tour guide is dedicated to inclusivity, so that all people feel welcome and valued.
- **Receptivity:** A good tour guide is a good listener, reflective, and open to change.
- **Flexibility:** A good tour guide is able to adapt and adjust when necessary.

Can you see how well this model adapts to the classroom? In our classrooms, these ideas help us co-create curiosity by harnessing our own passion and enthusiasm in a way that stimulates our students' curiosity. Therefore, our teacher tour guide job description might read something like this: "Must have a willingness to explore new ways to facilitate learning, take risks in teaching, and give up the compass when necessary." Some of the ideas may be uncharted territory for you, but one of the best ways to support curious children is to be curious yourself. We hope you'll be curious enough to try these ideas and approaches in your journey to become a tour guide teacher:

> **Investigate the teacher:** Abby loves starting the first day of school with a little surprise and curiosity through an "Investigate the Teacher" activity, where students search her classroom for clues about her passions, personality, and teaching style. This alternative to the traditional "Get to Know Your Teacher" slideshow gives students a chance to make inferences about her passions. By flipping the script in this way, Abby can build relationships and community from

the start, and it opens the door for her to share more about her passions throughout the year.

Lesson inspiration: If you're looking for creative lesson inspiration, start with what you know and love. Perhaps you're an avid sports fan, a nature-lover, a food connoisseur, or a fitness fanatic. Whatever you personally are curious about makes a great model for your students and might make lesson creation a little easier. A great example is Ashley's famous literary yoga lesson. She took something she is passionate about (yoga) and used it as an inspiration for a literary analysis lesson. (You'll learn more about this lesson in Inspiration.)

Displays: Another way to share your passions is through low-maintenance but high-impact classroom displays. For example, you could add a "What I'm Reading" note on the board with a picture of the cover of the book, or you could display several books on a shelf with a note that says, "I recommend." Instead of or in addition to sharing a book, you could also share and display relics of your favorite hobby, passion, mantra, quote, film, etc. Demonstrating that you are a lifelong learner in any capacity is a great model, and it can co-create curiosity for those students who might be interested in learning more about the topics you share.

Book talks: After making a connection between the books her husband reads and the books her students were carrying around, Jenna discovered the value of his book talk strategy (her husband is a government and history teacher at her school). A book talk is a simple strategy in which the teacher shares what they're reading. After finishing a book, Mike always brings it to school with him to show students the cover, read them the description, and then give his impressions and share what he learned. Modeling his own curiosity shows that he is curious and sparks curiosity for some of his students as well, thus co-creating curiosity.

Think aloud: A think aloud is an intuitive way to model your own thought process as you work through a lesson or activity with students. It is a specific modeling activity with the benefit of talking through your thought process. As you read a picture book, annotate a passage, work through a math problem, or demonstrate a science experiment, you'll explain what you're doing, why you're doing it, and how you're doing it in first person. Here's an example of a think aloud for an analysis of the picture below:

The first thing I notice is the way the boy stands out as the focal point of the picture. I wonder why he's in outer space. Could it have something to do with his space helmet? Wait! His space helmet is connected to a book, almost like it's feeding into his thoughts. He definitely looks happy about it, because I can see he's smiling and looks content. It's interesting that his eyes are closed as he's smiling. That tells me he's thinking about the book—or what's in the book. OH! Maybe it's a book about space! Aha! The book is taking him on a journey, maybe even a journey to outer space! That's it! Books can take you anywhere!

Embrace the rabbit hole: While we wrote this section on curiosity, we made a joke that we've never been more curious. Each new idea about curiosity led us down new rabbit holes, sometimes spiraling into hours of thinking, discussing, and writing about topics for this section that never panned out. Though we definitely had moments of frustration in the midst of our looming deadline, in the end, we realized that we did this section right! The whole point of curiosity is to go down those rabbit holes, even when it's frustrating to do so! For a fair warning, the last method for co-creating curiosity can be challenging, but ultimately, it can be so valuable for both you and your students. Embracing the rabbit hole means that you have to be willing to go down those rabbit holes with your students, even when it changes your schedule, reroutes your weekly lesson plans, and leaves you with more questions than answers. Here are couple of practical ways to embrace the rabbit hole and walk the fine line between frustration and fruition:

- **Research together:** You can go down that rabbit hole with your students and research together. It's so rewarding to watch students find the answers to their own questions.

- **Value voices:** Take student input to guide the direction of your classroom inquiry. We'll go into this much deeper in the section on freedom, but for now, just open your eyes, ears, and hearts to student interests and use those voices to guide your planning.

Now, let's turn to a very special classroom narrative from our friend Staci Yamanishi, an educator from the Los Angeles area. Staci demonstrates the magic of co-creating curiosity while honoring her family history and encouraging her students to do the same.

WONDER MAKER

STACI YAMANISHI (@DONUTLOVINTEACHER)

YOU'LL NEVER GUESS THE GEMS THESE STUDENTS UNCOVERED!

I was leaving school to make a twenty-four-mile roundtrip drive up and down the 110 freeway to pick up my grandma, all during my fifty-minute prep period. In Los Angeles, that's a bold move—traffic is *extremely* unpredictable. However, this was a special day. My grandma, Emiko Takusagawa, was going to spend the afternoon as a guest speaker in my eighth-grade class, sharing her experiences as a teenager during World War II.

On the drive to pick her up, I thought about my first memories learning about Japanese and Japanese-American incarceration camps. I couldn't pinpoint one specific moment, but I thought about how I helped stuff, seal, and address envelopes for veterans' organizations my grandpa participated in. My late grandpa,

Hiroshi Takusagawa, proudly volunteered for and served in the all-Japanese-American 442nd Regimental Combat Team, all while his family was unjustly incarcerated. He spent time sharing his story and advocating for the preservation of this history. I didn't ask all at once, but I definitely had a lot of questions.

Traffic was on our side, and my students would soon ask some of the same questions I had growing up. My grandma sat nervously in front of the class, slowly twisting back and forth in the chair. She was less afraid of sharing her experiences and more worried about the thirty-six sets of eyes on her. I could sense her discomfort. She always said that public speaking was more of Grandpa's gig. My grandpa taught me that we can't leave it up to others to tell our stories, and telling them will help prevent history from repeating. I quietly wondered to myself if my grandma was thinking about his words at that moment, too.

As my students asked questions about my grandma's experiences, I anticipated hearing a handful of familiar stories. I imagined she would share the challenging memories of burning family photographs soon after Pearl Harbor was bombed. I expected her to share that on the bus ride to Manzanar, one of the ten incarceration centers, she peeked out the covered window and saw what she would describe as the beautiful Red Rock Canyon formations. And she did.

What I didn't expect was that through my students' curiosity and questioning, I would hear stories, new to my ears, that would deepen my *own* understanding of my family history. *Can you share more about the things you took and had to leave behind? How was school different for you in Manzanar?* Through these questions, my grandma reminisced about her younger brother's bicycle and her fancy typewriter—gifts they received for Christmas just months before. Both were special things that were initially left behind, but were later returned to her family while in Manzanar. She described a range of topics from not having the opportunity to learn algebra to how she met my grandpa. Most importantly, she shared parts of my own family history that I would not have otherwise known.

Of course, everyone loved my grandma. When the bell rang, several students stayed behind to thank her, give hugs, or even just squeeze in another moment with her. When guest speakers are invited into the classroom to speak about their experiences, it creates a space for students to practice asking authentic questions. It models interview skills so they can continue this work by asking similar questions of the people around them. In search of their own histories and identities, my students uncovered family and community members who shared stories of everything from how they met famous individuals to someone who served meals to soldiers during the Mexican-American War.

On the drive home that day, I was struck by just how unpredictable learning can be—kind of like an unpredictable freeway. In hopes of helping my students gain context and empathy for my grandma's experiences, I too was leaving with new understandings. We never really know what our learning journeys will look like when we take time to ask questions, embrace curiosity, or invite others into the classroom, but the long route will *always* be worthwhile.

CURIOSITY DROPPED OFF A GIFT FOR YOU. OPEN IT UP TO SEE WHAT'S INSIDE!

Even if you don't think you're curious, the good news is *you already are*. We know it because you're reading this book in your spare time. But we also know it because humans are natural "informavores," creatures who hunt and gather knowledge. Curiosity is hardwired within our minds. We are born with the desire to explore the world around us, contemplate its endless questions, and relentlessly chase the answers. This precious little evolutionary trait could be our best-kept teaching secret, and it's time to unlock its magic.

While we hope the information and strategies we've offered in this section help you pass on your curiosity to your students, we want to remind you that you already have everything you need to teach students to be curious: *you.* All you need to do is lead the way and invite your students to join your adventure. As their tour guide, the best souvenir you can leave them with is the gift of curiosity. It's contagious, infinite, and self-sustaining, the fuel to fire a lifetime of learning.

We challenge you to have the courage to be curious in all that you do, but especially in your teaching. Never stop asking questions, challenging the status quo, exploring new ideas, and experimenting with different teaching strategies. Always mind the gap between *what* and *what if, why* and *why not,* and *today's* events and *tomorrow's* unknown. In the spirit of curiosity, we'll leave you with these questions that we can't resist contemplating:

- What if we valued curiosity just as much as work ethic and intelligence?
- What if we recognized it as one of the most powerful teaching strategies we have in our toolbox?
- What if we were more deliberate about cultivating curiosity in our classrooms?
- What if schools approached curiosity with the same dedication we devote to standards, data, and testing?
- How would a society full of curious observers, questioners, thinkers, debaters, and lifelong learners change the world as we know it?

ELEMENT 3
FREEDOM

*⌃Abby

I remember the first time I drove across the country by myself. A Midwesterner born in Ohio and living in Indiana, I had never been west of the Mississippi. The morning of my trip, I loaded up my little Civic with two weeks' worth of clothes, camping gear, and lots of snacks, taught a whole day of high school classes, and giddily power-walked out of the school doors as soon as the clock struck contract time. It was a Thursday afternoon, and I had thirteen hundred miles to cover before Friday night. Nineteen hours of driving stood between me and watching dozens of hot air balloons drift above the desert at the International Balloon Fiesta in Albuquerque.

I was exhausted from packing and teaching, and a little terrified about driving cross-country by myself. What if my car broke down? What if I got lost? What if I didn't make it in time? The what-ifs were overwhelming, but as soon as I pulled out of the parking lot, my fears eased, making way for the sweet euphoria of freedom. Besides my goal of making it to New Mexico by Friday night, I had no deadlines, no obligations, and no restrictions: just two weeks of fall break and a very loosely planned cross-country road trip. My itinerary, if you could call it that, was a messy Google doc of the national parks I wanted to visit, the campsites that I probably should have reserved, and one or two hotel bookings that I figured I should make so I could shower once in a while. I had "planned" my trip to be unplanned and flexible. I wanted the freedom to be spontaneous and make pit stops and detours on a whim.

And that I did. Even though I had fourteen hours of driving to cover on Friday, I casually exited the interstate to check out a stretch of the historic Route 66 in Oklahoma. Hours later, I stopped to see the famous spray-painted Cadillacs as the sun set over the golden fields of Amarillo. When I finally arrived in Albuquerque, I marveled at how I could be teaching in the cornfields of Indiana one day and then be in the desert of New Mexico the next. It felt surreal, as if I had been transported to an entirely different world.

To borrow a word from the state's motto, I felt enchanted. I was the happiest I had been in a long time. I went on to travel nearly five thousand miles across New Mexico, Arizona, California, Nevada, and Utah on that first trip, and as soon as I made my way back to the Midwest, I was planning my next adventure. I had fallen in love with cross-country road trips and the satisfaction of being here today and there tomorrow.

For me, this gratification comes from driving to my destination, rather than flying. I'm not content with the bird's-eye view out the window seat, nor do I enjoy all of the rules and restrictions of airports. No, I'd rather take control, make my own route, and drive. There's something magical about driving on an open road, an ever-expanding frontier of possibility. On the road, I can watch the landscape change from flat fields to rolling hills that give way to fiery-red rocks. In the car, I have a guaranteed front-row seat to the sunset every night. I have the power to take a spontaneous detour and happen upon a hidden gem that changes the course of my journey. When I'm in the driver's seat, I feel unconfined, alive, and euphoric. In these moments, I am free.

In a letter published in Jon Krakauer's *Into the Wild*, Chris McCandless wrote, "There is no greater joy than to have an endlessly changing horizon, for each day to have a new and different sun." When I'm weighed down by stress, monotony, or too much structure, I feel the pull of the open road, the endless horizon, and the new and different sun. I am tempted and delighted by the reminder that I could be in one place today and in a seemingly different world the next. My car keys feel like a little superpower hidden in my pocket. If I really want to, I can get in my car and just drive . . .

While I wish I could indulge in a spontaneous road trip every time I get the itch to jump in the driver's seat, I think my love for the open road is a reminder of the power of freedom. To reach your destination all by yourself, in your own time and on your own terms, is incredibly rewarding. Knowing you have the freedom to explore your world, embrace its surprises, and follow your curiosity is liberating—life-changing, even.

But this satisfying freedom should not be limited to road trips and breaks from school. It should be bubbling up and springing forth from our classrooms because our students deserve to experience liberation in learning.

★ ★ ★

At first, freedom will feel like a delightful surprise to your students, a deviation from the norm. In fact, many of the flashbulb activities we described in Surprise are fleeting doses of freedom. Similarly, curiosity is closely related to freedom: it's all about embracing the unknown and exploring the world around you. Freedom, you see, is the key to it all.

To sustain the engagement sparked by surprise and cultivated by curiosity, we must turn to freedom. Freedom is the master key that will unlock intrinsic motivation, epistemic curiosity, self-actualization, and joyful independent learning. In other words, freedom is the difference between engaging our students and empowering them.

When we turn over the key of freedom to our students, we will watch them unlock doors we didn't even know were there. But to free our students, we must free ourselves first. This means giving up the control that comes from a teacher-centered classroom and shifting to a student-centered paradigm that encourages choice and independence.

CHAPTER 10

FREEDOM TO LEARN

The concept of student-centered learning isn't new, of course. In fact, in 1969, Carl Rogers, one of the founders of humanistic psychology, switched gears to speak to educators. He wrote a foundational work to student-centered instruction called *Freedom to Learn*, which outlines a humanistic approach to education. Despite the fact that this work was written over fifty years ago, it's apparent we're still dealing with "The Dilemma" that Rogers outlines in his introduction: rote learning versus experiential learning. Rogers writes:

> I believe that all teachers and educators prefer to facilitate this experiential and meaningful type of learning, rather than the nonsense [rote] type. Yet in the vast majority of our schools, at all educational levels, we are locked into a traditional and conventional approach which makes significant learning improbable if not impossible. When we put together in one scheme such elements as a prescribed curriculum, similar assignments for all students, lecturing as almost the only mode of instruction, standardized

tests by which all students are externally evaluated, and instructor-chosen grades as the measure of learning, then we can almost guarantee that meaningful learning will be at an absolute minimum.

Sound familiar? One reason that Rogers's words strike a chord more than fifty years later is thanks to the influence of fellow psychologist Benjamin Bloom. Bloom, a behavioral psychologist, emphasized stimulus-based learning. In schools, we so often hear reference to Bloom's 1956 taxonomy of learning that you likely know it by heart. But remember that rote learning Rogers chastised? That's largely thanks to Bloom.

Bloom's taxonomy indicates that rote memorization is the easiest type of learning. Although our goal as educators is to move students past lower-level thinking, the instructional methods of behaviorists—rewards, motivation, and reinforcement—are very much present in schools. This creates what Brazilian educator and philosopher Paulo Freire calls the "banking model" of education. This traditional education system sees teachers as the bank. Teachers have all of the coins—knowledge. Their job, then, is to deposit their coins into the minds of the poor pupils whom they gift with their knowledge.

Clearly, there are so many problems with this analogy, yet as Strickland and Strickland describe in *Engaged in Learning*, "In traditional classrooms the teachers are the holders of knowledge, and it is their job to transmit this knowledge to students, who are expected to sit still, not talk unless called on, and concentrate on instruction that many find boring and frustrating."

Like Rogers, psychologists from other disciplines, such as cognitive and developmental, challenged this model. The student-centered instructional approach was born. Based on this approach, our philosophical goals for education focus on a constructivist approach, a model that promotes the *transaction*, or flow, of knowledge between the teacher and students, rather than *transmission*, to facilitate learning.

Embracing a student-centered model of instruction can be challenging because it does require you to relinquish the perceived "control" of a traditional, teacher-centered philosophy. But there's something magical that happens when a teacher steps back so that students can step in. Sometimes, when you do a little less, you make room for the students to do more. It's the difference between lessons and learning experiences, between engagement and empowerment.

Just like carefully "minding" the curiosity gap, this kind of approach requires a delicate balancing of structure and freedom. It takes deliberate design, thorough scaffolding, and repeated practice to give the students the reins—but once they have them, they can run.

Like classroom management expert Harry Wong says, "Whoever is working is the only one learning." We say this not to discount all of the hard work you do on a daily basis, but as a reminder of the power of student-centered instruction. It may sound too simple, paradoxical, or too good to be true, but we firmly believe this is where the wonder happens. When students are the ones thinking, choosing, experimenting, discussing, wondering, and working, they are learning.

Freedom is a powerful element that can be a source of empowerment, strength, and self-direction. And yet, as we're aiming to unlock windows and doors to wondrous learning, there are structural systems built right into our classroom walls that threaten to lock out wonder. As we consider the element of freedom, we must work to counteract those forces and keep inclusivity at the forefront of our instruction. Let's start by considering the Universal Design for Learning (UDL) framework by CAST, a nonprofit education research and development organization that works to expand learning opportunities for all individuals.

WHAT IS UDL?

The beauty of UDL is that while it provides a structured framework, it is very much like a road trip customized for each student. CAST organizes the guidelines for UDL into three categories: engagement, representation, and action and expression.

Here are some questions and considerations for each category as we prepare to reflect and plan the perfect learning experience for our students.

ENGAGEMENT

The UDL guidelines categorize engagement as our "why" of learning. When we think of engagement, we often think about hooks and getting students excited to learn and engage with the content at the beginning of the lesson, but we also have to dig deep to determine what makes them intrinsically motivated. Consider these questions as they relate to engagement:

- Do you consider students' interests?
- Do you communicate the "why" of the lesson?
- Is there student choice?
- Is your classroom atmosphere conducive to learning and free of distractions?
- What strategies do you have in place to promote sustained effort and interest?
- Do you use any self-regulation tools for students to analyze their own work?

REPRESENTATION

Similar to how engagement is the "why" of learning, representation is the "what." As we teach and provide materials and resources to students, are we considering the learning needs of all students as we deliver instruction?

When we think of representation, consider these questions:

- Are there alternatives for auditory and visual information?
- Can students customize the material?
- Are multiple media used?
- With new vocabulary, do you incorporate visual, nonlinguistic supports?
- Do you identify patterns between previous learning and future learning?
- Are there options to transfer and generalize this new learning in the future?

ACTION AND EXPRESSION

With action and expression, we move from the "why" and the "what" to the "how." How will students demonstrate their understanding of the material?

Some questions to reflect on with action and expression are the following:

- Are there any physical barriers?
- Are there multiple means and tools available?
- Are there multiple ways and methods to complete the assignment?
- Are assistive tools and technologies incorporated and/or accessible?
- Is scaffolding in place?
- Are graphics, organizers, and templates used to aid in retention and application?

Let's take a look at an example of when Staci used the UDL process to reflect and improve a lesson to make it more accommodating for all learners.

Staci

When I first learned about UDL, I used it to reflect on who I am as a learner. Take a moment and consider who you are as a learner. What engages you? How do you prefer materials to be represented? If you had a choice in how to complete an assessment, what would you choose first?

Over the years, I have taken a few online classes, and I struggle every time. I learn better through face-to-face interactions and lessons. I also have an extremely difficult time listening if there are no visuals or captions to accompany audio, so combine my lack of focus and the lack of visual tools, and it's a recipe for a very distracted Staci.

For one of my graduate course assignments, we were charged with picking a lesson and analyzing it through the lens of the UDL framework. I picked a lesson in which we read the short story "The Scarlet Ibis" by James Hurst and worked with a strategy called "Reading like a Writer."

If you're not familiar with "The Scarlet Ibis," it is a story rich with symbolism, character development, and universal themes. It teaches us a valuable lesson about how pride can drive us to make decisions with grave consequences. It also compels us to realize the innate beauty of the world around us and the people and animals within it. In this case, it was the beauty of the scarlet ibis, a bird, and Doodle, one of the main characters, who left us in awe.

Realizing those lessons and feeling that awe occurs because when we read as readers, we focus on ourselves and for the enjoyment and connections we feel to a text. Using the Reading like a Writer strategy, we can hop inside the mind of the writer to question *how* and *why* they made that happen for us. That's where the Reading like a Writer strategy comes into play.

Check out the chart below to see some of the questions we might ask ourselves when we switch between these two reading approaches.

Reading like a Reader	Reading like a Writer
• What do you **feel**? • What can you **infer**? • What can you **predict**? • What **questions** do you have? • What **connections** can you make? • What is your **reaction**? • Do you **agree/disagree** with what's happening in the text?	• What **words** does the author use? Why? • What **narrative devices (similes, metaphors, description, characterization, foreshadowing, repetition, etc.)** does the author use? Why? • What do you **know** about the writer?

When students see the strategy presented in such a way, they can begin to understand and appreciate more about an author's craft and purpose. You'll see another example of this later in Inspiration through a vignette shared by one of our Wonder Makers, Vennieta Grant.

After reflecting and analyzing my lesson based on the UDL framework and questions we reviewed earlier, here's what I found.

ENGAGEMENT

I used some of the ideas we mentioned in Surprise and Curiosity to hook and engage my students: an engaging first slide displayed on the screen, ambient sounds of nature filling the classroom, props ready to teach symbolism, and more. While I did the frontloading of engagement work and had my classroom ready to pique their interests, I realized that after I assigned the graded portion of the lesson, the Reading like a Writer annotations, I did not provide any self-evaluation work, nor did I provide a rubric for the assignment. Providing a rubric or even including a visual point breakdown on slides can be especially helpful for students to self-monitor their work and to keep them engaged with the process.

REPRESENTATION

Before we started reading, we discussed symbolism, because "The Scarlet Ibis" has a key symbol: the ibis. To review symbolism, I presented students with the written definition and then various examples of ways we see symbols in our daily lives and in literature. We looked at social media icons and what they represent and talked about how certain colors represent different ideas. Afterward, I pulled random items out of a suitcase (yes, that same one from the What's in the Suitcase? activity) for them to identify the item, its literal meaning, and its meaning in literature.

When it came to the actual reading of "The Scarlet Ibis," students had the opportunity to read the story through the textbook we had in the classroom, listen to the audiobook version, and/or use the online PDF to read the story. With these options, they could control the rate of reading, zoom in on the digital options, and highlight.

Providing multiple means for learning symbolism and multiple options for accessing the text was a good start; however, I found that the audio accessibility was lacking in that it did not have closed captions on-screen. Many students used headphones and followed along with their print or digital copy of the story, but having the words on-screen is beneficial. I also realized that in this one lesson, I introduced a lot more vocabulary than I had thought, so some previewing of the vocabulary and activating their prior knowledge would have been a more inclusive and proactive step for me to take.

ACTION AND EXPRESSION

For the Reading like a Writer annotations, students chose to complete their annotations in a range of formats: on paper or Post-its if they did not want to use technology, and in Google Slides or Google Docs if they did. I had a digital template ready with sentence starters, and if students chose the digital version, they could use speech-to-text instead of typing.

After reflecting on this lesson again, I realized that I was providing a variety of options for writing, but how important was it that the annotations be written? Could I have provided opportunities for students to record their annotations in a video or options for verbal or visual expression? According to the UDL guidelines, part of analyzing our action and expression work also asks us to "provide alternatives in the requirements for rate, timing, speed, and range of motor action required to interact with instructional materials, physical manipulatives, and technologies." If I required four annotations, how important was/is it that *all* students have four? If a student could show mastery with two, did I need four? Could I provide more time for students?

Reflection is one of the very first steps you can take to free yourself so that, in turn, your students can be more empowered with the direction of their own learning. As your reflection translates into more student-centered approaches and activities, your students will be ready to unlock even more of their potential.

★ ★ ★

We'd like to end this chapter with a powerful narrative from Tanesha Forman, a former teacher and current middle school principal in New Haven, Connecticut. She is an educator committed to social and racial justice, and simply put, her narrative shows us the power of freedom to learn.

WONDER MAKER

TANESHA FORMAN ( @LOVETANESHA)

In the middle of our class discussion, I glanced at my students. Bobby had a stony stare and pursed lips. Ajani must've noticed his demeanor, too, because before I could engage, she invited him into the conversation. She turned to Bobby and asked, "What are your thoughts on what *Copper Sun* teaches us about ways Africans endured or resisted their enslavement?" He sucked in a deep breath, peered into Ajani's eyes, and retorted, "They ain't do enough. They didn't resist. The characters suffered in the book, and Black people are still suffering." I scanned the room for reactions. There were nods, snaps, claps, eye rolls, and sighs. A few students looked to me for a response, but this was their conversation.

Silence enveloped the room for a few weighty seconds. Ajani spoke up and said, "I hear you, but they did resist. The ancestors were strong. Jumping from the ships was resistance, singing was resistance, learning English was resistance, and remaining connected to their land and values was resistance." Bobby replied with a cold, "Yeah, how did that help them?" Once again, there were nods, snaps, claps, eye rolls, and sighs. Rejinae asked, "Does resistance only matter when it's connected to getting something?" I couldn't help but snap and scrunch up my face in that "you go, girl" type of way.

Bobby chirped in, "Yeah. Why else resist?"

With the second question, multiple students started to speak, but D'Andre's words rose to the top, and everyone else paused and listened. He said, "The act of resistance is about defiance and letting people know you matter. Throughout history, and in this book, we have examples of how Africans resisted. When Amari learned English, she was resisting, because language would give her access to knowledge that could free her from her captors. This was true for our African ancestors. When she demanded to be called by her name, she resisted because she was holding on to who she was and to hope. That's what the resistance of Africans was about. Hope is what sometimes gets us through, right?"

D'Andre was looking at me, but Bobby piped in with, "I feel you. Sometimes hope is all we got." In response, there was a round of snaps.

The conversation continued to flow for another five minutes as I stood back and witnessed the power of discourse. At the end of class, I sifted through student responses to our closing question about what lesson we could apply to our lives based on the text and discussion. Several students wrote about the power of hope. I landed on Bobby's response. He wrote, "Life as a young Black kid ain't easy, but I don't have to accept that. I can fight back in small and big ways." I smiled, shook my head, and whispered, "You go, boy. Yes, you can."

CHAPTER 11

FREEDOM TO EXPLORE

When was the last time you explored something new? Like, really explored it, every nook, cranny, crack, and crevice? Think back to your childhood, when you excitedly scouted all of the slides, swings, bridges, and tunnels of a new playground and plotted out how you'd explore each part. Remember what it felt like when you perused each and every shelf of your first book fair, fascinated by pages and pages of possibilities.

Now, fast forward to the time when your teacher journey began. Recall the thrill of rummaging through a teacher supply store as you shopped for your future classroom. Relive the moment when you finally unlocked that very room and explored the maze of hallways in your new school.

Surely you know the feelings: the electricity that runs through your veins as you explore something for the very first time and the delight that comes with discovering your own path. Are these feelings limited to these nostalgic moments, or are they alive and well in your own classroom? Do your students have the freedom to explore and follow their passions?

This may sound like overwhelming, uncharted territory for you as a teacher, but the journey to joyful autonomy begins with small steps. Freedom to explore is all about listening to your students, providing choice, and fostering exploratory learning.

Before we embark on this journey together, let's take a look at how Jenna followed the compass to freedom in her own classroom.

⋆Jenna

Think back to high school for a minute. What was your *Moby Dick*?

Of course, I mean that novel that you absolutely detested, couldn't bring yourself to read, or just flat out thought it sounded awful.

For me, it was *Moby Dick*. For Abby, *Great Expectations*. For Staci, *The Odyssey*. For Ashley, *Brave New World*.

If you would have asked me at the time, I'm certain I would have begged for the freedom to choose another book. I loved reading; I just didn't like *that* book.

What about kids who just don't like reading at all? How can we help them learn to like it?

As a new teacher, I pondered these questions, but without good answers, I resorted to what I knew: assigning books from the canon that my school provided all the while ignoring that faint voice of my former 16-year-old self saying, "Give them choice."

I went right on assigning whole-class novels that I know did not appeal to all students (because, well, that's impossible). All the while, I continued to wonder, *Will this book be their* Moby Dick? Some bolder students answered this question loud and clear.

To counter their disinterest, I'm embarrassed to say that I resorted to antics, accountability quizzes, and threats to "motivate" students to read the book. In "Farewell to *A Farewell to Arms*: Deemphasizing the Whole-Class Novel," Douglas Fisher and Gay Ivey sum up exactly what I was doing:

In the hope that students can be coerced into reading a novel that they have been assigned, teachers often resort to testing their knowledge about it. Some teachers give oral summaries of the contents so that students who have not completed their assigned readings can 'keep up.' Others show the film version so that students have a sense of the content. Regardless of which alternative is selected, students are not reading more or reading better as a result of the whole-class novel. Instead, students are reading less and are less motivated, less engaged, and less likely to read in the future. Meanwhile, teachers continue their endless—and often fruitless—search for better ways to persuade students to read their assigned novel.

For years, I justified these behaviors as a necessary part of the game, convincing myself there was no other way.

Alas, there is a better way, and it all starts by stopping the justifications and listening to the kids instead—the ones in your classroom and the one you used to be.

Change didn't happen overnight. I went from canonical whole-class novels units to carefully curated book lists to full-on freedom to choose. It's taken time—almost a decade—and I'm still learning, experimenting, and adapting. But each step toward freedom to choose is a step to open shiny glass windows to a world of new voices, identities, and experiences, to create heroic, powerful, and joyful reflections for students to see themselves. And it all started with a tiny first step: listening.

★ ★ ★

In 2010, Patall et al. did just that. They conducted a study with two groups of students: group one had choice on their homework assignment, and group two did not. After switching the control and test groups, they reported key results: choice matters! Not only were students more motivated to complete the assignment, but they also performed better on the unit exam.

This study only confirms what you know or guessed. So the question is, "What do you do if you don't have autonomy, or even a little wiggle room, in your curriculum or reading selections?" We realize it's not a reality for everyone, as it hasn't always been for us. It's frustrating, and it can easily lead us to a place of defeat. Don't give up. No matter the situation, we can make responsive pedagogical decisions that empower our students. Here are ways that we've adapted our curriculums to meet the needs of all students:

Short works: If you can't replace a unit, as Staci explains in depth later, you can always supplement an existing novel unit with short works. Similarly, graphic novels and memoirs also provide short yet poignant ways to provide windows and doors to new perspectives. Marjane Satrapi's *Persepolis*, George Takei's *They Called Us Enemy*, and Art Spiegelman's *Maus* are examples of graphic texts that could supplement historical and cultural study lessons in humanities classes.

Multiple perspectives: After researching multiple perspectives in the secondary ELA classroom for her dissertation, Jenna adapted the schools of literary criticism into digestible literary lenses for her students. When studying a work of literature in her classroom, she creates activities for students to try new lenses of interpretation. Even with the classics, there is room for diverse perspectives! Here's an example: As an option for *Of Mice and Men*, Jenna suggests engaging students with close reading activities related to multiple perspectives. Specifically, she challenges students to analyze the work with reader response, social, historical, critical race, women's studies, and critical dis/abilities studies lenses. These lens activities encourage students to explore new interpretations and reactions to the text.

Text pairings: Pairing a prescribed whole-class novel or textbook with young adult novels, nonfiction articles, documentaries, dramatic films, and podcasts can create opportunities for rich discussions about different and often conflicting perspectives in the text. Once restricted to a British literature curriculum, Ashley brainstormed creative ways to pair diverse selections. For example, when teaching *The Canterbury Tales*, she paired the concept of language change and the skill of code-switching. When teaching "A Modest Proposal," she prompted students to research social justice topics and choose an issue to voice their own stylistic proposition. When approached from a cross-curricular standpoint, text pairings can provide dynamic content to better reach all student interests.

Independent reading: While you advocate for better books and a more responsive curriculum, one way to immediately implement change is through an independent reading program. After she accepted a new position and reviewed the limited choices in the book cabinet, this is what Abby did to ensure that her students had access to stories that mattered to them. She helped students register for free digital library cards through the public library and showed them how to use the website OverDrive and the Libby app to access e-books and audiobooks. By using the public library, partnering with the school librarian, featuring high-interest books, and giving students time in class to read, Abby has prioritized independent reading in her curriculum. Even if you don't teach ELA, you can still enrich your content area with independent reading. By giving students a key to all the books in the library, you open up a world of choices to explore for any interest or subject area.

Whether you have free rein or little leeway with your curriculum, there's always room for improvement. For a practical yet powerful example, let's take a look at how Staci adjusted a district-required unit to make it more responsive to her students.

Staci

In an interview, Nic Stone, author of *Dear Martin*, recalls the books she read as a high school student. She remembers that she met three African American characters, and "all three characters were written by white authors. And none of them got to be heroes."

When I read Stone's descriptions of these books, I instantly recognized them, because not only had I also read them as a high school student, I taught them as well, and in these books, there is no joy, no triumph, and no celebration for these Black characters.

I knew that I had to make some changes to the texts I taught in my classroom. In my district, we have a few target text options to choose from for each unit, but we also have some flexibility with the texts, as long as they relate to the unit's themes/standards and offer text complexity.

I began asking teachers for short story suggestions, and I also found resources from Lit C.I.R.C.L.E. (Curriculum for the Inclusion and Representation of Communities of Color in Literacy Education). From there, I started planning how I wanted to replace *Of Mice and Men*. During the summer, I teach a six-week course for the Upward Bound Math-Science program at the University of Delaware, where I have complete autonomy, and I created a unit using the following short stories:

1. "The 'F Word'" by Firoozeh Dumas
2. "Girl" by Jamaica Kincaid
3. "Thank You, Ma'am" by Langston Hughes
4. "The Bus Ride" by Sahar Sabati
5. "The Stolen Party" by Liliana Heker

Throughout this unit, we focused on theme, author's craft, writing strategies, character development, and more, much like I had done with my *Of Mice and Men* unit in previous years.

On average, we read one short story per week, and whether it was Dumas's experiences with moving to the United States from Iran or Hughes's tale on the power of mercy, these stories allowed us to have rich discussions about various cultures and humanity while still discussing and meeting the themes, concepts, and standards of the original unit.

After seeing the success of the unit in my summer class, I knew it would be a hit with my students at my school as well.

★ ★ ★

In addition to rerouting your instruction so that it's more responsive to students' needs and identities, it's important to give students time to engage in their own exploration. Not only will they be exploring their own topics and texts, they'll also be exploring themselves. As ELA teachers, we know that much of this is rooted in reading, but these strategies can be applied to all subject areas, because literacy is the key to it all.

> **Brochure browsing:** Staci loves using book tastings in her classroom as a way to get students to "taste" some new books, and brochure browsings are a great spin-off of this activity that you can use with shorter texts, such as articles. Staci sets the mood with some dim lighting, cookies and snacks, and café music in the background. The goal is to provide students with an opportunity to browse short pieces of writing and explore their contents like you would if you were reading a brochure. Students can make note of the headlines, leads (opening lines), images, captions, titles, text structures, features, and more. What she'll do is place a variety of articles

from different sources on the tables, and students can spend a few minutes browsing their "brochures," snacking away and embracing the coffee-shop vibes, all while recording their observations.

Reading raffle: Reading raffles are a perfect way to build excitement around free-choice reading no matter what grade or subject you teach! Ashley first discovered this activity from elementary classrooms and quickly realized how well it works in secondary settings too. Build excitement around free-choice books, magazines, or podcasts by first displaying and talking up the selections. Next, make sure each "prize" has a vessel, such as a cup or envelope displayed with it. Then, let students add their names to the vessel for a chance to win first dibs at checking out a book, reading a magazine, or listening to a podcast with a special headset. Lastly, make a grand occasion out of drawing the names and announcing who "won" (just be sure to have consolation prizes on hand such as a library pass, older-edition magazines, or regular headphones). This fun process can be repeated throughout the year, and teachers can capitalize on seasonal interests, such as hosting a spooky reading raffle in the fall. The theme possibilities are endless and are sure to make students feel extra lucky about their freedom to read what excites them!

Choice challenges: Jenna creates reading challenges to encourage her students to explore new perspectives, and this type of exploration works well for enrichment in any discipline. Students can explore different branches of scientific research in your science class, weekly wellness readings in your health class, important mathematicians in your math class, or new genres in your English class. You can create whatever parameters you need, but then let students get to work to finish each requirement before the end of the semester or year. As the year goes on, don't forget to share your own progress with students. This is a good way to remind them to stay on pace with their challenge. Plus, it's a great way to get you involved as well!

Quick clips: Abby uses Book Trailer Tuesday to help her readers discover new books, but the concept can also be used to encourage other kinds of exploration. With a little bit of your own searching, you can find quick clips that feature topics, texts, people, or fun facts that relate to your content. Whether it's a *2 Minute Classroom* video, historical fiction book trailer, current events, or a TED-Ed lesson, pressing play can be a quick way to spark students' curiosity. To maximize the impact of this strategy, quickly survey students after each video to gauge their interest, and give them the opportunity to submit ideas for future video topics.

Whether you're offering choice or encouraging exploration, freedom is as simple as listening and responding to the students in your classroom. Let's take a glimpse at how Ashley did just that.

⋆Ashley

Though I am still in the process of working to provide equitable choices for all students, I can tell you about a pivotal moment in my journey. I was a brand-new teacher doing an old-school research paper in the library with my senior British Literature students. Per tradition that I never once thought to question, students were tasked with researching and writing about one influential Brit who made an impact on the world at large.

I passed out a passed-down handout with a long list of famous British figures and gave students ten minutes to add a star by someone they were curious about. However, one of my students didn't need nearly that long. After her quick scan, she raised her hand and asked, "Mrs. Bible, are any of these people Black?"

> Me (panicked and embarrassed): "Um, I'm not sure. Let me look ... "
> Me (reading the list frantically while the class looks on): "No, I'm sorry ... I ... uhh ... "
> Student (trying to save me): "Can I just pick my own British person to write about?"
> Me (relieved): "YES!!! I would love that!"
> Student: "OK, who are some famous Black British people?"
> Me:

Just thinking about this story ten-plus years later makes my face burn with shame. However, rather than replying something defensive like, "This is a research project; go research!" or delegating like, "That sounds like a job for the librarian; go ask her!" I simply replied that I didn't know and that was my fault. I told her that we would research together because she sparked my curiosity and inspired me to expand my knowledge. She respected that, and essentially, this is what I've been doing ever since.

I actively seek out the resources by educators of color, research how to reach all students, and expand my classroom walls to the world around us.

Nowadays, that old-school research paper looks a lot different, but with each new unit I create, I hear that student's voice checking in on me to ask what students will see on the pages I assign. When I give students freedom to explore, I strive to make sure choices are inclusive and exciting for all students!

It is our hope that you are reading this book of your own free will. That you picked it up because it interested you and because it sparked your curiosity about keeping the wonder in education. However, if you are here because a well-meaning administrator made you read it or because you feel obligated by an outside force, does it hit a little differently? Don't answer that. Well, do answer it, but only in your head as you reflect on how you as an educator interact with pedagogical content you had the freedom to choose versus content you were forced to consume. Which do you enjoy more? Which do you engage with more? Which do you learn from more? No matter why you are reading this book, we hope that we have inspired you (in one way or another!) to add more freedom to explore in your curriculum.

CHAPTER 12

FREEDOM TO DISCUSS

Walk into any school cafeteria, and once you get past the ear-splitting sound of chatting and chewing, you'll find a world of highly engaged, highly responsive students. If you take a stroll past the table on the left, you might hear a heated discussion about the best Avengers movie. The table on the right might be discussing the steps to choreograph a TikTok dance. Compare this to the common classroom scenario where you try to elicit responses to a lesson by asking, for example, "So, what themes do you think we can express from this work?" (Internal dialogue: Wait time . . . 1 . . . 2 . . . 3 . . . 4 . . . Ugh!)

Hand goes up.

Instant relief.

"Thank you for volunteering *again*, Jane."

From the teacher's perspective, this experience can be so disheartening. *Why won't they just participate? Are they even listening to me?* You can threaten them with participation points. You can call on them in order. You can beg them. You can rely on your trusty hand-raiser. Still, more often than not, these trials can leave you feeling frustrated, betrayed, and inadequate, and the truth is we've all encountered this situation at some point in school, either as a student or a teacher.

So where did this very traditional and often-used model go so wrong? Well, let's start with the obvious: you'll notice that the "discussion" is completely teacher-centered. The teacher was asking a question and eliciting a response in a big group (presumably a whole class) and looking for *one* response (the *right one*) from *one* student. This is hardly a discussion. In fact, it sounds a lot more like a lecture.

Even though this is the method most of us experienced in our formal education, it's not exactly the most traditional method out there. In fact, there is one method that predates our schooling experience by a long shot, and you've probably heard of it before because it's named after its creator. It's called the Socratic method.

It should come as no surprise that we're back to citing Socrates, whom we dubbed the father of wonder, and who most famously rejected the lecture model of his time. Rather than sitting at the front of the room and projecting his wisdom on his students, Socrates would walk around the room and ask question after question. Students were so engaged in this method of rapid-fire questioning that a passionate debate among students ensued. Socrates's point was to encourage students to challenge their thinking. This method of instruction, now commonly used in law schools, encourages students to use advanced critical thinking skills to find meaning through contradiction. Relating to primary and secondary discussion strategies, the tour guide teacher we identified in Curiosity can invite and engage students down this same path.

Just like Socrates, we invite you to step out from behind the podium or desk, symbols of authoritarian teaching. Keeping in mind our ideas about classroom setup, you'll create a physical space where walking around the room to engage with students will feel natural and welcomed. Building this classroom community can seem daunting and even haphazard, but it provides a pathway to freedom to discuss.

PARTICIPATION PATHWAYS

I was once on an interview panel for hiring a new teacher in our school district. I have to admit that I was so excited to be a student for the day during the lesson demo—that is, until I was called on to read a vocabulary word, then panicked, mispronounced the word, and never lived it down from our former ELA teacher, who was a school board member! (The word was *sinew*, pronounced "sin-EW," not "SEE-new," like I flubbed.)

That situation reminded me just how hard it is to be a student in class. Lots of students are reluctant to answer questions, yet when we're pressed to lead a class discussion, it's a teacher's nature to resort to calling on students. What's worse is this method of cold-calling is often encouraged by administrators to ensure student engagement.

In his article "Your Hand's Not Raised? Too Bad: I'm Calling on You Anyway," educational researcher and lecturer Alfie Kohn challenges this practice, saying:

> I'm tempted to ask a cold-calling teacher, 'How would you feel if an administrator (at a faculty meeting) or a speaker (at a workshop) did the same thing to you?' But that's not really the right question because some teachers are sufficiently comfortable in the spotlight that they wouldn't mind. The point is that lots of adults, and even more kids, *do* mind. Our obligation is to imagine the perspective of the specific person with whom we're interacting, not our own likely reaction in their situation.

The truth is, at the beginning of my teaching career, Kohn could have been talking to me. I was a cold-calling teacher. It wasn't until I read the book *Quiet: The Power of Introverts in a World That Can't Stop Talking* by Susan Cain that I realized the effect of this strategy on our classroom community.

This book helped me see non-hand-raisers in a completely new light. In the introduction, Cain attempts to define introversion and extroversion only to concede that personality types are so complex that psychologists have varying definitions. (I also learned that an ambivert is a person who is equally introverted and extroverted. I've considered myself an introverted extrovert since I took my first personality test in high school. Therefore, interestingly, I believe I fall into this category, and maybe you do, too.) Cain made me realize that not all classroom participation should be judged by how comfortable someone feels speaking in front of a large group.

If you need further evidence, take this excerpt from a speech by my former high school student Mackenzie. She wrote this speech during her freshman year of college (she graciously gave us permission to share it here):

> Since the first day I started school, every teacher I ever had used the same word to describe me: quiet. It was not uncommon for one of my classmates to come up to me and ask, "How come you don't talk?" It felt like everyone looked at my "being quiet" as a stifling medical condition. One that prohibits the ability to communicate and speak freely. One that doctors refer to as introversion.
>
> My whole life, I have put myself down for being an "introvert." I always wished that I was more talkative, that I was more outgoing, and that I wasn't referred to as boring. Last year, however, I finally learned not to be so hard on myself for being quiet, and I owe it all to my senior year English teacher.

My senior English teacher was the first teacher, and really the first person, to speak of "being an introvert" in a positive way. She admitted that she used to think that introverted students don't participate in class, and aren't engaged. But she took the next step that most people don't. She researched introversion. She shared her findings with the class, and explained that introversion is NOT a bad thing, and that introverts ARE participating in class. They just participate in a different way. Ever since then, I have been able to start accepting my quiet personality, instead of hating myself for it.

★ ★ ★

Considering all of this powerful evidence, we believe the goal of our classrooms should be to create a culture that provides pathways to freedom-to-discuss opportunities for all students with different comfort levels and abilities. Here are our suggestions for establishing freedom-to-discuss opportunities for your students:

> **Set guidelines and expectations together:** One of the ways we can provide freedom to discuss is by establishing roles and expectations together. This is particularly important for small-group discussions and one-on-one conferences so there is accountability for all members, including the teacher. In fact, setting expectations is sometimes the most important part for the teacher. It's challenging for us to step out of the role as leader, but given the opportunity, students can step into this role and find their voices in surprising ways. Also, this act can create an accountability piece to assist you in providing a fair assessment of the discussion. Sometimes evaluation of a discussion is necessary. Self-assessment, which will be discussed in detail in the next chapter, can be

a great piece of this puzzle. But it's sometimes not enough to be the only piece, as educator Robert Probst admits: "We do need . . . some way of encouraging students to take classroom conversation seriously." Probst suggests we "try to articulate for ourselves and our students just what it is we're hoping for in classroom conversation."

Move to small groups or one-on-one discussions: Moving to a small-group or conference model can definitely benefit all students, especially those who are less inclined to speak in front of the entire class group. Within those small groups, setting expectations for each member can provide accountability. For example, students can choose which questions they will be in charge of facilitating or leading. Other students can record insights when they're not the leader.

Give students time to prepare: After students understand and are aware of the discussion opportunities and expectations, give them time to prepare. This will prevent them from feeling put on the spot, and it helps them develop richer conversations.

Reframe your questions: The way we ask a question really matters. One example is the "Do you have any questions?" question. When we ask a question this way, it often puts students on the spot to say yes or no. To say yes means being singled out and could make them feel like they are an outlier among all of the students who just got the lesson. When we reframe the question to "What questions do you have?" now we are inviting and encouraging all students to ask questions. It's amazing how that one little shift can encourage so many more valuable questions.

Listen (really listen) to student response: Sometimes when we're looking for a specific answer, it's easy to discount students' insights. The shift in questioning should help us avoid this altogether, but that doesn't mean that we won't have to retrain our thinking. Strickland and Strickland give great advice to practice nonjudgmental listening: "To improve the listening aspect of our teaching, we can practice saying back what the [student] said ('What I hear you saying is . . . ')."

Let's look at an example of how Darrian Tanner, a Florida high school English teacher, instructional mentor, and author, creates a classroom culture that provides freedom for all students to participate.

WONDER MAKER

DARRIAN TANNER (@TEACHMSTANNER)

"All right, class. We're going to have our first discussion assignment tomorrow," I said to my tenth-grade English class. In the midst of the array of excited responses with a few "ah mans," I couldn't help but notice the saddened expression of a student I'll call Joseph. Joseph was an extremely quiet but pleasant young man, so this was new. The bell rang, and Joseph started collecting his stuff rather slowly. When he got up to go, I asked him to stay behind.

"Joseph, what's the matter? Why are you so sad?" I asked.

We sat there for seconds before he answered, and at that moment, it dawned on me that I never really heard him speak.

"I can't," he said.

"What do you mean?"

"Ms. Tanner, am I going to get a zero?" he asked with a slight stutter.

"You don't want to do the discussion tomorrow?" I asked.

"I want to, but I can't," he said. Tears started rolling down his face. This was my first time seeing a student cry. He proceeded to tell me that he had a terrible childhood experience that left him unable to really "think and speak."

"My brain is bad," he said. I followed up with his mom, and she did indeed confirm that there were some major challenges with Joseph's ability to process and explain his thoughts. She never did offer much clarity on the childhood experience, but I could see the struggles. And of course, I told him that he could write his thoughts instead for the assignment. That night, the educator in me reflected on my principle of creating a classroom culture that allowed all students to be a part of discourse in the class—to have a voice and contribution in discussion.

I took out a white blank index card and wrote a small affirmation for Joseph to say every day to build his confidence in thinking and speaking. We started out saying it together, and he eventually started saying it on his own. Then a couple of months later, during a classroom discussion, I took a risk and asked, "Joseph, do you have anything to add?"

He looked at me. There was a long pause, but his classmates were very patient and respectful. And then came out of his mouth the most profound thoughts about Martin Luther King Jr.'s "Letter from Birmingham Jail"—so profound that they carried the rest of the discussion. After much encouragement and support, Joseph became more and more talkative in the class until he almost took over the discussions. But it was a great experience that taught me a lot. I still see his face and the smile he gave after he spoke for the first time in class. A smile of freedom in his ability to learn, understand, and contribute.

STUDENT-LED DISCUSSION MODELS

Now that we understand the pathways for transforming our classroom culture, we can use the Socratic seminar discussion model as a starting point for developing expectations, guidelines, and an accountability piece. A Socratic seminar, naturally named after Socrates, is a student-centered approach to discussion in which students support each other in their understanding of a text, theme, or topic. What's great about this model is that you can adapt it to work for your classroom when you co-create the specifics with your students. Here are our tried and true Socratic seminar models that provide wonderful opportunities for freedom to discuss:

> **Fishbowl discussion:** A fishbowl discussion is a play on the traditional Socratic seminar that involves inner and outer circles. (A circle desk or table formation is a common setup for Socratic seminars to indicate equality.) The inner circle is "in" the fishbowl carrying on the discussion, while the outer circle silently completes their roles. The outer circle, for example, can take notes or participate in the color-coded silent discussion that Ashley will explain later in this list. Jenna likes to ask the inner and outer circles to switch roles halfway through so everyone gets a chance with different participation roles.
>
> **Socratic soccer ball:** If your goal is to quickly engage students in a discussion or get them out of their seats during a prolonged learning session, then Socratic soccer ball is a perfect tool to have on hand! Ashley simply used a marker to write open-ended questions on a soccer ball and has used it to block boredom ever since. The prompts include wording like:
>
> - How does the author demonstrate _____?
> - Elaborate on _____.
> - How would the story be different if_____?
> - Can you list three ways _____?

To participate, students simply toss the ball to a classmate in the standing circle. The catcher can read any prompt that the hand touches. The student reads aloud: "What can you infer about _____?" Then, the teacher finishes the prompt and allows the student to answer. The teacher finishes: "What can you infer about the character's remark in the section we just finished?" The student then discusses this prompt. If other students want to elaborate, they can ask the catcher to pass the ball after they have finished their point. Since this strategy is fast-paced, some students may need more thinking time, guidance from the "coach" (you), or to pass the ball without answering. Remember, the main goal of this activity is to add a little play, movement, and energy to a lesson, not to expose or embarrass students who require more thinking time.

Silent discussions: Nonspeaking chats are important because they give pensive, shy students a chance to shine while mandating more thinking time for outspoken, domineering students. There are several ways to conduct a silent discussion. For example, Ashley utilizes technology by creating a collaborative document with premade columns and rows. In the first column, she provides a space for students to type their name in a unique text color combination. One student may choose a purple font highlighted in yellow. Another student may select a blue font highlighted in pink. The goal is for each student in the document to have their own unique color-code. Following the discussion principles above, students then type their first discussion question into the second column. Next, students silently reply to the questions they are most interested in within the question column using their color-coded responses. Not only do students enjoy seeing the novelty of their classmates writing in real time, but the end result is a rainbow of responses that provide a visual representation of how the conversation progressed and what revelations were made.

Panel discussions: To combine the concept of a small-group discussion with whole-class engagement, try a panel discussion. Modeling after academic and political panels, Jenna modified the format for her classroom. Her students' panel discussions involve a small group of four or five students and a moderator. The moderator (a teacher or another student) poses open-ended questions related to a text, theme, or topic. The panel responds with an internal discussion. The rest of the class participates as an audience simultaneously using Ashley's color-coded digital silent discussion to carry on a discussion related to the panel's discussion. This is a great way to engage all students in a variety of roles. You can have students rotate in and out of the panel discussion or create groups of different panels to add further dynamics to the conversation.

Speed discussions: This is a simple discussion strategy that involves quick rounds of one-on-one discussions or debates. For each rotation, students are paired up with a new partner and challenged to answer a new question or discuss a different topic. This structure gives students the opportunity to critically think, hear different perspectives, and articulate their ideas in a low-risk, student-centered setting. Abby loves using speed discussion to help students synthesize ideas during thematic units or to encourage collaborative brainstorming during the pre-writing stage of the writing process. She also uses a variation of speed discussion, "speed debating," to help students strengthen their persuasive skills.

★ ★ ★

Staci

During my first year of teaching, I learned a valuable lesson about the power of a single conversation. Little did I know that one seemingly simple question would be the catalyst for that realization.

Naturally, as a new teacher in the building, I had students and colleagues who wanted to get to know me, and if you know anything about teenagers, you might guess that one of their first questions was "Ms. Lamb, you got a boyfriend?"

I always responded, "No." No, I did not have a boyfriend. I had a girlfriend. Technically, I wasn't lying when I told them no, right? However, I realize now that the larger question they were asking was "Are you in a relationship?"

One day, one of my colleagues and I were sitting in our collaborative planning room when she asked, "So what does your boyfriend do?" Instantly, my adrenaline started running, and I could feel the redness in my cheeks. I avoided answering with a pronoun, just as I had done so many times before, and said, "Works as an accountant."

I sat there for a few moments, struggling with what I had said versus what I wanted to say, when I finally broke the silence: "I actually have a girlfriend."

I was met with something immediately after that terrifying moment: relief. A sense of freedom. I realized, "Yeah. I can talk about this now. I'm comfortable here." I told that one colleague, and then, after that, I told my other colleagues. From there, I joined the GSA Club as an advisor, and that's what led me to have even more fruitful discussions with those students, including one who sent me this email (that I will absolutely treasure forever) during Teacher Appreciation Week in the middle of our first COVID-19 closure:

> As a young queer person, it is so meaningful to see queer adults and to see that despite the statistics, it's possible to live past eighteen . . . Coming to high school and seeing

that it's not only the white [cisgender] gay men who are already more represented in the media who can survive gave me hope. Knowing that there can still be a diverse community of people in the real world was really reassuring and validating to me. The fact that you're out is also so inspiring because I know just a few years ago, I thought that I would have to hide my true identity in order to get anywhere in life. Plus, you're an activist, constantly advocating for the community and amplifying the voices of other marginalized groups including ones that you aren't a part of. I see so much ignorance from other students when it comes to things like racism, so it meant so much to me when we were able to have that one conversation in GSA about the heated online debate you got into. It really made me feel like I wasn't alone, and I didn't have to be the only one who knew racism existed.

What that student didn't know is that, like him, I thought that I had to hide my true identity, but the collective, reflective experiences I had through powerful, open discussions allowed me to reflect on who I am and who I will be.

As you prepare for your first or hundredth discussion in your classroom, I encourage you to always remember this: never underestimate the power of an inclusive classroom and the power of an inclusive space to have discussions. Whether they are Socratic or silent, small-group or whole-group, teacher-led or student-centered, the discussions in your classroom will be that much more powerful if your students know that they have a safe and welcoming space to do so.

CHAPTER 13

FREEDOM TO ASSESS

As English teachers, we've fantasized about cloning ourselves, hiring a grading assistant, or finding a cute little robot to automate the seemingly endless tasks of providing feedback and assessing student work. While we wish it were as easy as saying, "Alexa, grade my papers!" the reality is that assessment is a daunting task, one that can take away our time and freedom outside of school.

What if you could share this workload, improve student feedback, *and* make formative assessment more meaningful? What if you could do less but accomplish more? It may sound like a riddle, but there are solutions that do not involve contemplating the ethics of human cloning. Thankfully, the answer is simple: shifting the ownership to students.

After all, if we are embracing a student-centered, wonder-filled approach to education, shouldn't our key stakeholders have a genuine role in assessment? Why should we work hard to provide students with choice, tap into their interests, and cultivate their curiosity, only to abruptly abandon our philosophy when it's time for an assessment, evaluation, or grade?

Our students deserve the freedom to assess: the opportunity to make judgments about their work and use this kind of evaluation to propel their learning forward. We're aware that there are often many external forces exerted on our assessment practices: standardized testing, district-mandated assessments, antiquated grading systems, and more. But we also know that formative peer- and self-assessment are free, powerful tools that every teacher can utilize, no matter the environment.

PEER ASSESSMENT

Whether you call it peer review, peer editing, peer feedback, or peer evaluation, peer assessment is a powerful strategy that shifts students from passive to active participants in their learning and paves the way for later self-assessment. To clarify, given the different names for similar concepts, we define peer assessment as any activity that asks students to evaluate a peer's work with clearly communicated or co-created criteria.

Many teachers shy away from peer assessment because of the fear that students may do more harm than good, or because of a painful memory of a disastrous peer-feedback flop. Such concern and trepidation are understandable because peer assessment requires the teacher to rethink traditional practices and give up a degree of control. In other words, it means treating students as the stakeholders that they are and empowering them to learn from each other.

In a meta-analysis of peer assessment studies, Double et al. found that peer assessment improves learning in primary, secondary, and higher education. According to their findings, peer assessment was more valuable than no assessment and teacher assessment. For those worried about the reliability of peer assessment, an earlier meta-analysis by Nancy Falchikov and Judy Goldfinch found that peer grades "agree well with teacher marks on average." Best of all, peer feedback promotes evaluative judgment and self-regulation, two skills that experts argue are crucial for lifelong learning.

In other words: Peer assessment *works*. It's worth any of the discomfort that comes with giving your students the reins, red pens, and rubrics. With the right structure and scaffolding, peer feedback can be a transformative strategy.

Let's examine a few factors that make certain models of peer feedback more effective than others:

- In *Teaching in Higher Education,* after analyzing different models of peer assessment, researchers concluded that peer feedback works best when students receive verbal, in-class, face-to-face feedback from more than one partner.

- According to Falchikov and Goldfinch, the most reliable peer assessment involves holistic evaluation. Because of this, they promote an approach of using criteria to arrive at an overall judgment, rather than specifically evaluating each criterion.

- Finally, for peer assessment to fulfill its formative purpose, students must be given time to utilize peer feedback and revise their work before teacher assessment.

It's important to note that peer assessment is most successful in a classroom environment where students feel safe, trusted, and empowered. Additionally, students will benefit the most when peer assessment is a valued, repeated, and natural part of learning, rather than an occasional, isolated activity.

Here are a few of our favorite ways to incorporate peer assessment:

> **Peer feedback speed discussion:** This strategy is Abby's favorite way to engage students in formative assessment during the writing process. It is a method of peer assessment in which students rotate through mini peer-feedback sessions. During each round, students switch partners and discuss a different

guiding question or element of the work. For example, for feedback on an essay, the first round might focus on the hook, the second on background information, the third on the thesis statement, the fourth on the first topic sentence, and so on. This scaffolded, structured approach breaks down the daunting task of peer editing and helps students stay focused. Instead of reading a peer's essay from start to finish, students can focus on small, manageable sections and strengthen their editing endurance. To maximize the impact of this strategy, use guiding questions, checklists, rubrics, sentence starters, and other tools to help students craft quality feedback for their peers. Here are the guiding questions Abby uses for the first few rounds of peer feedback speed discussion:

- Does the writer include a hook? Does the hook engage you and make you want to read more? If not, offer suggestions for how to reel readers in.
- Does the writer bridge the hook to the thesis with background information on the topic? Does the bridge offer sufficient information to introduce a reader to an unfamiliar topic? If not, explain what readers may need to know.
- Does the writer present a clear, arguable thesis statement at the end of the introduction paragraph? Does the thesis present a unique perspective on the topic? Can you tell what the essay will address? If not, ask clarifying questions and/or offer suggestions to make the thesis stronger.

Self- and peer-revision stations: Once a peer-review critic, Ashley now refuses to grade essays unless they've been through these self- and peer-revision stations. The key, she has found, is to incorporate tech revision tools and teacher input into the peer review–station mix. As groups of students rotate through the stations every eight to ten minutes, they will get professional grammar advice from smart and free programs like Grammarly or ProWritingAid, along with feedback from peers. But most importantly, peer review–station day ensures that every single student receives a micro-conference with the teacher. Though this station is only eight to ten minutes long divided by each person in the rotation group, approximately two focused minutes on a single paragraph can work wonders in advancing student writing through personalized instruction. Since the other stations focus on grammar, word choice, peer editing, and formatting, the teacher-delivered station is designed to provide time for micro writing conferences that take young writers to the next level.

Sticky-note peer review: If digital peer review isn't an option for your students or assignment, you can mimic this procedure with sticky notes. First, give each student a number. Then, ask students to use their numbers on their submission instead of their names. If they already have their names on their submissions, you can cover it with washi tape; it peels right off afterward. Then, add two sticky notes to each essay with the corresponding number. Randomize essays and ask students to give feedback right on the sticky note. It's a good idea to collect the sticky-note feedback after round one, so the next reader isn't influenced by the first score. At the end, you can stick the feedback right on the essays. Sticky notes add a bit of novelty, and they're convenient for you to collect and redistribute.

SELF-ASSESSMENT

For our purposes, we will define self-assessment as a type of formative assessment that asks students to self-evaluate their progress and use their reflection to move forward in revision and learning. Research has shown that self-assessment is a transformative strategy, one that can unlock intrinsic motivation, a sense of internal control, deeper learning, metacognition, self-efficacy, and ultimately improved achievement.

In "Student Self-Assessment: The Key to Stronger Student Motivation and Higher Achievement," James H. McMillan and Jessica Hearn outline the three components of the "cyclical, ongoing process" of self-assessment:

- Self-monitoring (awareness)
- Self-judgment (evaluation of learning)
- Learning targets and instructional correctives (taking steps to improve learning)

For this model of self-assessment to work, McMillan and Hearn stress that teachers must provide clear learning targets, model the progression of learning with proficiency-based rubrics and exemplars, and give students the chance to revise after self-evaluation. While self-assessment may be the key to more active, engaged learning, we can't throw our students in the driver's seat and expect them to navigate the new territory of self-evaluation without directions. While empowering, this kind of autonomy will initially feel daunting or uncomfortable for students. The first time we ask them to assess, they may miss the mark and overestimate their learning or judge their progress too harshly. Reaching genuine self-assessment takes dedication, time, and practice.

So just how can we help our students practice their evaluative skills? For starters, you'll need to clearly communicate learning goals and *the language of assessment* to your students. This means familiarizing them with the rubric and using it as a learning tool, rather than a grid of boxes that reports a final grade. We recommend introducing the rubric to students at the beginning of a unit, referring to it throughout, and giving them multiple opportunities to practice using it. Here are some ways to do just that:

Model self-judgment skills: You can do this by showing students examples and "thinking aloud" as you explain how you would evaluate the quality of work with a rubric. Brownie points if you model using your own writing or work. The more transparent and vulnerable you are, the more students will learn that critical self-assessment is a natural part of the learning process.

Facilitate small-group peer feedback on sample work: After modeling, this is the next logical step in an "I do, we do, you do" approach. For example, provide groups with sample essays and a copy of the rubric. Then, ask them to read, debate, and evaluate the essay with the rubric before coming together for a whole-class discussion. The small-group, low-risk setting will allow students the opportunity to flex their judgment muscles without worrying about grades. In addition to small-group sessions, you can also incorporate activities where students rank, sort, or organize examples of work, justifying their judgments.

Incorporate multiple opportunities for peer review: To accurately judge the quality of their own work, students will need to become more familiar with applying the rubric and/or criteria for feedback. Naturally, this exposure and practice work well in a peer-to-peer setting. Once again, keep peer review low-risk and structured enough to provide students with guidance.

Invite students to assess you: Give students a chance to practice their peer feedback skills by "grading their teacher" with the rubric or criteria. The novelty of this experience will engage them, and students will feel free to be critical and observant if you emphasize that this is a no-risk opportunity to stick the standards to their teacher.

Introduce self-assessment in small, manageable chunks: Once students have had plenty of practice assessing their peers and sample work, you will need to ease them into the intimidating task of assessing their own work. For example, if you are teaching writing, ask them to assess one element of an essay: perhaps their thesis statement, their topic sentences, or their evidence. In addition to this kind of scaffolding, consider using other tools, like checklists, sentence starters, question stems, and graphic organizers.

Provide feedback on students' progress and evaluative skills: Empower students with feedback that will move their learning forward. To do this, focus on the learner and the process, rather than the work itself. Part of this includes offering feedback on students' self-assessment skills. Feedback "should perhaps focus less on the quality of students' work and more on the fidelity of their judgements about quality," according to Tai et al.

Conference with students: Monitor students' progress and the growth of their self-assessment skills with guiding questions during one-on-one conferences. Here are some example questions:

- What have you learned that will help you the next time you do this?
- What is one area in which you can grow as you continue to work on this?
- Now that you've worked on [skill], what is your next goal?

At its heart, self-assessment is an incredibly simple strategy; it requires minimal prep, no additional tools, and common-sense pedagogy. With repeated practice, it can become a natural, intuitive part of the learning process. This is why we love self-assessment: It will take students farther than you could on your own. It has the power to transcend the walls of your classroom, empowering your students with self-efficacy and unlocking the door to independent, lifelong learning.

I experienced the synergy of freedom, curiosity, and surprise when I sought to teach my senior Technical Communication students how to design and deliver an engaging slideshow presentation. After witnessing one too many occasions of a student reading black Times New Roman text off a white screen with no visuals, I blocked off two weeks for a "Slideshows That Don't Stink" mini-unit. But when I sat down to outline the final assessment, a slideshow presentation, I was stumped. I didn't know what to "assign" the students. What would they research? How could I give them some structured choice under some kind of umbrella topic?

After agonizing over the parameters of this assignment, I finally decided to give my students none. No restrictions. No suggested topics. Nothing, except for the good old "school appropriate" clause. (Yes, I did have to clarify that when a student wanted to research pickles because of their phallic shape.) The only thing I encouraged them to do was find a weird, obscure, or random topic—the last thing they ever imagined they would research for a high school assignment.

After all, I was assessing them on their ability to deliver a visually appealing, informative, and engaging slideshow. The content did not matter. When I explained this project to my students, they were surprised, curious, and even a little bit overwhelmed by all of the freedom I had given them. But after some brainstorming, my students decided on some ridiculous topics: mole rats, honey, paper clips, and chicken wings, just to name a few! They were so amused by the novelty of it all that it motivated them to do their topics justice by researching them with a renewed sense of curiosity that I've never witnessed in students plagued by "senioritis."

I even encouraged a bit of friendly competition among students and encouraged them to really "sell" their topic to their peers. "How are you going to make paper clips seem as cool as chicken wings?" I would joke. I would creep on my students' screens through our Chromebook monitoring software, laughing out loud as they created their slideshows on milk and shoelaces. My students were having so much fun that I even got a little bit jealous, so I did the project myself. Yes, I wanted to "model" with a "mentor text," but I also just wanted an excuse to create and deliver a totally weird slideshow. I decided to research the common loon, an aquatic bird known for its interesting calls, and when it was time for me to model my presentation, I passed out rubrics and let my students "grade" me. They thoroughly enjoyed the freedom of assessing their teacher (and some even gave me C's just for the fun of it), but more importantly, this helped familiarize them with the expectations and rubric.

As I laughed my way through the student presentations (because it's hard to take a slideshow about mole rats seriously), I was blown away by how much they had learned and how much we all had enjoyed this project. Even the student who had quite literally not completed an entire project all year created and delivered a presentation. I'll never forget that group of students and how much we bonded over our shared curiosity for loons, paper clips, and chicken wings.

CHAPTER 14

FREEDOM TO PLAY

"No, Joy!"

★Ashley

As anyone who has ever loved a pet can attest, losing one leaves a hole in your heart disproportionate to the physical size of even our biggest furry friends. In one of the most challenging seasons of my teaching career, I helplessly watched my beloved dog Hank fade from cancer, along with my creative classroom spark. It was at the end of this gruesome and miserable semester that a flash of light beamed in the darkness. In fact, it was the light of my phone screen, which lit up a Petfinder notification at five a.m. on the last day of school before our holiday break. Though we never thought we could welcome another dog into our lives, the moment I saw this precious pup named Joy as a Christmas-themed adoptee, I knew she was meant for our family.

The allure of that adorable furry face in the adoption photo is how my husband and I went from being seasoned pet parents of our late perfectly behaved angel to newbie dog trainers of an inexhaustible, irresistible, unpredictable bundle of Joy.

The rest of that winter break was challenging but so full of love and laughter. In fact, it led to a funny epiphany about pets, students, and life in general. You see, having a new puppy with the name of Joy made for some comical linguistics.

Want to sneak a snack off the counter? "No, Joy!"

Want to play past bedtime? "No, Joy!"

Want to give an overly enthusiastic greeting? "No, Joy!"

Want to break free and explore the world? "No, Joy!"

One snowy morning as I took Joy on her walk, I scolded, "No, Joy!" after she persisted in trying to eat jowls full of snow with every slushy step. This is when I suddenly realized the irony of her name paired with the happy-halting word she heard all too often. I laughed out loud as her big brown eyes stared inquisitively up at me trying to decipher my sudden change in mood.

I've since put a great deal of thought into responses and actions that look and sound like "No, Joy!" to students. If you put the word "joy" with these common student behaviors and requests, it's easier to realize that even with the best of intentions, the word "no" can be a real killjoy.

Want to listen to music? "No, Joy!"

Want to play a game? "No, Joy!"

Want to work in a group with friends? "No, Joy!"

Want a break to shake the wiggles out? "No, Joy!"

To create a joyful yet well-behaved classroom environment, think of ways you can productively orchestrate moments that allow you to say YES to classroom joys and personal freedoms.

MOVEMENT

One way to shape classroom joy is through movement. Not only is movement a key factor in creating a sense of bodily freedom, it's also essential for learning. Studies, like the one done by Joseph E. Donnelly and Kate Lambourne, show that physical movement activates the brain, creates stronger connections, and correlates with academic achievement. Through increased blood flow, improved oxygenation, and incredible nerve cell growth in the hippocampus, regular and extended heart-pumping exercise can actually change the structure of our brains to enhance memory, attention, and mood. In one inspiring study from the book *Spark: The Revolutionary New Science of Exercise and the Brain,* Dr. John Ratey describes a school in a suburb outside Chicago that implemented an intensive and measurable exercise program designed to ensure students meet their daily aerobic activity goals. The results were tremendous. As childhood obesity rates and stress levels went down, academic achievement and standardized test scores went up. However, unless you are a physical education teacher or launch an innovative school-wide exercise program, it would be difficult to reach the long-lasting, brain-changing level of exercise within your classroom walls.

Nevertheless, there's proof that simple classroom movement strategies can also boost mental performance. In a paper titled "Effects of a Classroom-Based Program on Physical Activity and On-Task Behavior," researchers described their findings that simple, short bursts of movement throughout the school day helped all students, especially students who were least likely to be on task. Results of a similar study published in *Preventive Medicine* called "Implementing Classroom Physical Activity Breaks: Associations with Student Physical Activity and Classroom Behavior" revealed that activity breaks reduce lack of effort in class and increase attentiveness.

Then there's the anecdotal evidence.

Ashley

Teaching seniors three weeks before graduation requires willpower, determination, and innovation. One year when I had exhausted these requirements, I tapped into my faithful friend, creativity. Tired of teaching ninety minutes of English literature to distracted, lethargic, senioritis-ridden students, I began brainstorming ways to wake up and shake up my lesson plans.

It came to me during my morning yoga routine. Feeling my energy rise during my sun salutation, I decided that a mid-class stretching break would work wonders. But as I continued to move and muse, an entire literary yoga flow took shape. Excited to try out my newly formed literary yoga routine, I queued up a soothing playlist and pounced at the first sign of reading "stag-mina." Simply adding an element of surprise by hitting play on windchime music perked the students up, but then they really became fully engrossed when I broke into a tree pose and instructed them to join in.

I said in my most calming yoga-teacher voice, "Trees are resilient. They can withstand outside forces because they are so deeply rooted. As you practice this balance pose, think about which characters in our story are resilient like a tree. What are the conflicts that test their resilience?"

There was laughter, there were concerned side glances, there were show-offs, but most importantly, there was energy! Whether they did the pose correctly or not, they were out of their desks and moving! We went through several other poses, such as flat back for flat characters, circle arms for round characters, triangle pose for plot diagram, and eagle pose for point of view. After our ten-minute movement break, students were more alert and focused than they had been all week.

In the study "Gesturing Makes Memories That Last," researchers found that when learners are asked to perform actions, they remember those actions better than if they simply talk about the same topic. When compared to no activity, movement leads to more robust learning and retention.

How can you add meaningful movement to your curriculum? Think about shapes the body can make to fit your content. For example, the plot triangle pose could easily be adapted into a triangle geometry lesson for math class, a rhetorical triangle for debate class, a shape lesson for kindergarten class, or a food pyramid lesson for health class.

Other Moments of Movement ideas:

Walk like Aristotle: There's a reason Raphael's fresco *The School of Athens* depicts Aristotle and Plato walking. Aristotle was a famous walker, often giving lectures and doing his best work during walks. Even his students and literal followers were known as belonging to the Peripatetic school—*peripatetic* derived from Greek and meaning "prone to walking about," especially while teaching or disputing. Science has since corroborated what Aristotle knew long ago: walking leads to increased creative thinking. In the report "Give Your Ideas Some Legs: The Positive Effect of Walking on Creative Thinking," researchers found that walking boosts creative ideation in real time and even prolongs residual creativity shortly after. With this in mind, Ashley prompts her students to walk like Aristotle around the perimeters of the classroom during moments that require creative thinking such as pre-writing brainstorming, debate preparation, or theoretical questioning.

Anticipation guides with a twist: Because of their reputation, worksheets can sometimes be a killjoy. In an effort to reduce worksheets while continuing to use anticipation guides to activate students' prior knowledge and build curiosity, Ashley made up a "Be Your Own Star" strategy. In his essay "Self-Reliance," Ralph Waldo Emerson begins with a quote from the stage play *Honest Man's Fortune*: "Man is his own star." Emerson then goes on to write, "To believe your own thought, to believe that what is true for you in your private heart is true for all men—that is genius." Playing off of "be your own star," Ashley instructs students to stand up and form a star with their body, legs apart and arms spread wide. Then she tells them to follow their own genius. Without worrying about what their neighbor is thinking, students tilt their "star" right to agree and left to disagree. For example, if you were standing in the star pose right now and were given the anticipation statement "If students are having fun, they aren't learning," which way would you tilt before reading this book and after reading this book?

Learning stations: Though we've mentioned them several times already, stations are the perfect strategy for giving students a sense of freedom through movement and independent tasks while also ensuring learning is being facilitated. Better yet, the small-group, low-risk setting of learning stations often gives a voice to students who may be uncomfortable in whole-group discussions. When Abby is searching for a way to flip a boring, teacher-centered, or stagnant lesson, she turns to learning stations. Instead of giving a lesson an extreme makeover, she is often able to simply repurpose and restructure existing content into student-centered stations. For example, Abby has transformed every single one of her former novel or literary movement introduction slideshows into stations that give students the chance to explore the content on their own first. While Abby does this with novels, you can do this with any unit introduction, whether it's a time period in history or a new topic in science. The best part is that after facilitating introductory stations, you will be better able to fill in any gaps in background knowledge and start your unit with a stronger foundation.

Four corners: This is an incredibly simple kinesthetic strategy to help students collaborate and critically think about multiple-choice questions. To do this, first designate and label the four corners of your room as A, B, C, and D. (If you need an E option, the middle of your room will suffice.) Then, show students a question and ask them to travel to the right answer, the right corner of the room. Once in their respective corners, students should discuss and defend the answer with their peers. After students have claimed their corners, facilitate a review of the question, but give time for students in the wrong corners to move to a new one. The kinesthetic element of this activity will make the "process of elimination" visual and concrete for students, who will quickly be able to narrow down the answers and arrive at the correct one.

PLAY

Imagine the surprise on Staci's administrators' faces when she told them that during an observed lesson, she was taking her teenagers down to the gym to play Hungry Hungry Hippos. After seeing Hope King do the lesson with elementary students, Staci had to try it with her freshmen. It was a risk for sure because, oftentimes, we equate play and too much fun with little instructional value. We stress about connecting the "fun" to the standards, when in reality there is so much value in the genuine act of play itself. As students raced around the gym with baskets, chasing hundreds of brightly colored balls that corresponded to review questions, the smiles on their faces told Staci and her administrators everything they needed to know.

The older we get, the less "play time" we tend to incorporate in our lives, but when does play start? In "The Importance of Play in Early Childhood Development," Anderson-McNamee et al. say play begins in infancy. Whether a baby is making random movements, grabbing that rattling object, or watching others play, this is when they begin to understand what play is.

Young children move from concrete objects to abstract fantasy play, and toward the preschool period, they move to cooperative play in which they are organized into groups and become aware of different roles. Here, they experience the many benefits of play: physical movement, discovery, creating bonds, and developing problem-solving, language, and social skills. Because of these benefits, play is crucial.

According to the researchers, seventy-five percent of a brain's development occurs after birth, and play helps to form the connections between nerve cells. These connections lead to the growth of fine and gross motor skills as well as language and socialization skills. Later in life, play helps children learn how to act in society and adapt to the ever-changing world around them.

Regardless of grade level, play is a component that we can always enjoy and benefit from. Here are a few ways you can incorporate the different types of play in your classrooms:

> **Motor-physical:** This category involves using fine motor skills to engage in play. While reading Shakespeare's *Macbeth*, Ashley had students create a tiny drama set out of random classroom objects and conduct a finger puppet play. Teams closely read their scene independently, deliberated on which lines were the most essential, worked together to translate the antiquated text into contemporary language, and then performed the play with their fingers as actors. The performances were both pedagogical and playful!

Constructive: After seeing her students' obsession with the Netflix show *Nailed It!*, Staci created a lesson on ethos, logos, and pathos by having her students construct their own gingerbread house. In a messy, playful environment, students worked either independently or with a partner to construct a beautiful creation and then convince their peers that theirs was the best one using the different rhetorical appeals.

Expressive: Expressive play allows for emotional response to flow throughout the activity and assignment. Take spoken-word art, for example. After her class read *Long Way Down* by Jason Reynolds, Staci had her students create their very own form of spoken-word poetry but also added an art element to it. Students could use various materials to create a visual product that complemented the content of the poem.

Fantasy: Fantasy play allows students to take on roles and act out different scenarios. This is one way that big and small kids alike can enjoy the benefits of non-realistic play. Students can assume roles from a story and recreate scenarios, or even better, they can invent a chapter, section, or revision. As a bonus, simple costume elements can make all the difference. Take Jenna's senior English class as an example. Students assumed roles of characters from "The Pardoner's Tale" from *The Canterbury Tales*. Donning makeshift costumes, they invented a courtroom scenario with several imaginative twists. This fantasy play required students to assume roles, envision new scenes in the story, and ultimately reimagine the ending.

Cooperative: Cooperative play allows students to work as a team with a common group goal and play games with rules. For example, students work together to review for an upcoming test by playing a variation of Guess Who? where they can role-play as different characters, other individuals, or even elements. For instance, in science class, students could take on the role of a part of a cell and interview each other to later determine how they work together. Questions, stems, or other cues can help students interact with each other during the game, and peers can guess who is who at the end of each round.

★ ★ ★

The electric energy in the hallways on the last day of school. The anticipatory stance in the aisle awaiting the deboarding process. The shiny key in the ignition celebrating an aced driving test. The thing all of these scenarios have in common is that they capture the giddy anticipation of exploration.

We savor these moments, but we shouldn't have to wait until the next break, trip, or celebration to revel in the joy of freedom. Instead, we can prick up our ears and listen to student voices as we open up our classrooms to provide learning choices. Once we learn to loosen our structured itinerary a little, we can create space to celebrate the identities, passions, and interests of our students as we forge a learning path together.

ELEMENT 4

INSPIRATION

Staci

What inspired you to become an educator? Some people have a burning passion to become educators; others choose it as a second career. And for some, like myself, becoming an educator was completely unplanned.

I always enjoyed watching *Matilda* growing up, and it wasn't until recently when I watched it again that I saw just how much I connected to the story and, in particular, the movie adaptation. In a world of chaos, Matilda found an escape through books and school. Like Matilda, I, too, traveled all over the world just by turning the pages of books, and from an early age, school was both an outlet and a motivator for me. Unfortunately, unlike Matilda, my telekinetic powers haven't shown up yet, but I'm still hopeful.

On my first day of high school, I eagerly scanned my schedule to see what my day would look like, and right at the bottom was one course I definitely hadn't signed up for: Air Force JROTC. I wasn't even sure what the program was, nor did I have any interest in a career with the Air Force, so my first thoughts were "How did this happen?" and "How can I get out of it?" Little did I know I would end up spending all four years in the program with instructors Major Steven Michael and Master Sergeant Leroy Rush.

Over our four years together, my instructors and I talked about everything from my home life to my future. When it came time to start applying to colleges and I chose international business as my major, Mr. Rush was hesitant: "I don't know if that's the right fit."

I didn't fully realize and appreciate just how right he was until after my first year of college, because trust me, I did not do well. I started skipping class, and my grades started slipping, too.

On my way home one day, I was on the phone with my best friend Justin. He reminded me of what I love doing: being creative, teaching others, volunteering, and being with people. When he said, "I think you should become a teacher," in that moment, I thought back on all of the teachers and school experiences that inspired me every day. Not long after, I changed my major to English education. From there, it felt like all of the puzzle pieces of my life started falling into place. I enjoyed going to class, I performed significantly better academically, and I felt like I had purpose.

Two years ago, I returned to my high school to visit, and one of my first stops was, of course, the Air Force JROTC room. As a teacher, I know how challenging it is to remember the names and faces of the hundreds of students we teach, so when Mr. Rush and Mr. Michael instantly recognized and hugged me, I was overwhelmed with gratitude.

We ended up chatting in their office, and I updated both of them on my career change. I shared with them my recent honor of being named the Teacher of the Year for my district. What was most powerful was when Major Michael said to me, "I wasn't sure if you were going to make it." And I knew what he meant: make it out of the poverty cycle, the stuck-in-that-hometown cycle, the could-be-lost-potential cycle.

What I hope I communicated in our meeting is that, in many ways, their class inspired me. The routine, the open communication, their stories, and their willingness to not ever give up on me inspired so much of who I am as an educator ten years later.

As I look back on my years as a student and now my eight years as a teacher and mentor, I see the role that we all play in each other's lives. I see the role of what a little dose of inspiration can bring and do for us. I see the connections, the possibilities, and the opportunities that education collectively offers us.

★ ★ ★

Education is an ongoing and ever-changing symbiotic relationship between all of us, with surprise, curiosity, freedom, and inspiration woven throughout. All of us were inspired to become educators in different ways: Ashley from giving computer lessons to senior citizens, Jenna by admiring her teachers and college professors, Abby after years of begging her four younger siblings to "play school" with her, and you for your own reasons. It's safe to say that, though our stories are each unique, no one feels inspired to become a teacher by reading through what seems to be one of the most focused components of teaching—a list of state-tested standards.

When we envision our best teacher selves, it looks like making life-changing connections with students, seeing the "aha" moments in real time, helping students discover their identities, and finding the sweet spot between a passion and a profession. It sounds like excited discussion, laughter from students "tricked into learning," and curious questions. It *doesn't* look like students taking standardized tests, and it *doesn't* sound like educational jargon.

In order to keep the wonder of education alive for ourselves and our students, we must learn to merge our pedagogical passions with mandated minutiae. In a world that values test scores and scripted curricula, we must learn to stay inspired and seek creativity instead of standardization.

How are you so creative?! I don't have a creative bone in my body. I wish I was creative like you! Where do you come up with all of these engaging lessons?

Throughout our careers, all four of us have heard variations of these questions and comments. While we identify as creative individuals, trust us when we say that creativity and its cousin, inspiration, can be just as elusive to us as they may seem to you. In fact, as we've written this book amid a global pandemic, we've experienced our fair share of creative ruts, writer's block, and unmotivated days, weeks, and even months.

So who are we to write a book on keeping the wonder and teaching with creativity? We are teachers who actively search for our inspiration, because we know it's out there. We are teachers who have trained our brains to jump-start our creativity. We are teachers who hunt for ideas in our experiences, on our bookshelves, and in the world around us. We are teachers who know that creativity is often not about entirely original ideas. Rather, creativity is about the sparks that fly between the ideas: synthesis. To create is to connect and combine, to blend and build upon, to rearrange and reinvent. Contrary to common beliefs, creativity is not the inherent gift to make something out of nothing. Instead, it's the freedom to create something out of anything.

So what does this mean for us? Inspiration is out there, everywhere. It's free, abundant, and always near. All we have to do is look.

CHAPTER 15

INSPIRED BY CREATIVITY

Every year, the World Economic Forum publishes the report *The Future of Jobs: Employment, Skills and Workforce Strategy for the Fourth Industrial Revolution*. Not surprising to educators, the 2020 report listed creativity as a core work-related cognitive ability among other related abilities: cognitive flexibility, logical reasoning, problem sensitivity, mathematical reasoning, and visualization.

The report defines creativity as "the ability to come up with unusual or clever ideas about a given topic or situation, or to develop creative ways to solve a problem." This definition sounds a lot like what we must do on an everyday basis as teachers. It also stresses that one of our main goals should be to teach students creativity in preparation for the workforce.

This leads us to an important distinction. There are two ways to discuss creativity for educators: (1) teaching creativity and (2) creative teaching. Teaching creativity means empowering students to be creative, and according to the National Advisory Committee on Creative and Cultural Education, creative teaching means "using imaginative approaches to make learning more interesting, exciting and effective."

So the question is, how can we harness both of these types of creativity?

Even if you don't see yourself as a *creative teacher*, you're probably more creative than you think, and you certainly have more potential than you've likely imagined. In fact, you've likely been misled by strict, traditional definitions that imply creativity is an innate gift reserved for a select few. While we think creativity will always be a little bit magical and elusive, we believe that it is within reach for *everyone*. Thankfully, cognitive science supports our suspicions.

Neuroscientist and executive coach Tara Swart reminds us that creativity is "not the traditional view of being good at art or full of new ideas, but it is the ability to shape our own brain by what we expose it to, designing our future through proactive choice." In her book *The Source*, she dismisses the myth of the left-brain/right-brain dichotomy, citing research that points to brain connectivity that "enables us to engage in both creative and analytical thinking." So if you've always seen yourself as a logical left-brainer, this is your permission to pursue creativity.

As it turns out, creativity may be more of a skill that you can practice rather than a fixed trait. One 2010 study by Fink et al. found that "cognitive stimulation via the exposure to ideas of other people" boosted creativity. Another study by Sun et al. that sought to build on the growing body of research by examining neuroplasticity found that "creativity training can reshape both the function and structure of the brain."

While researchers are still exploring the intricacies of our brain and how it engages in creative thinking, one thing is clear: you can train your brain to be more creative. We've found the best way to train our brains is through inspiration. Let's start with what inspired Ashley's creative teaching journey.

Ashley

It's the last day of school and I'm using our party day to finish up decorations for another joyous celebration—my wedding set to occur the very next day. Looking back, this was not my finest moment of planning, nor was it professional, but it did result in one of the biggest lightbulb moments of my entire career.

A few interested students gathered around my craft station, and we talked about my special touches for my extreme DIY wedding. As I was chatting excitedly, one girl squealed, "You are so creative! You should change professions!"

My face dropped. Years of conditioning had convinced that student (and me) that school, especially secondary school, was a place for seriousness and standardization, not play and creativity. Because of this, I was holding back our greatest gift—the gift that would benefit students the most, the gift that would bring joy to my classroom, the gift that would increase the longevity of my career. So the day before my wedding, I made a vow to myself and future students that I would not reserve my creativity or theirs for after-school hours. Instead, I would embed imaginative assignments into our lessons so that our creativity could flourish and shine.

Luckily, I was teaching in a school that welcomed innovation and creativity in both teachers and students. As long as I had my "why" in the right place, administrators gave me the autonomy to add more creativity (and the wildness that comes along with it) to my classroom! In the book *Creativity: Flow and the Psychology of Discovery and Invention*, author Mihaly Csikszentmihalyi explains that each of us is born with contradictory tendencies. There's a part of us that is conservative of our energy and risk and a part that liberally seeks novelty, exploration, and possibilities. From an evolutionary perspective, we need both of these tendencies to thrive. However, as Csikszentmihalyi explains, conserving comes more naturally, and if there are too many obstacles and too few opportunities, then the little spark inside of us that lights up when creative opportunities arise is all too easily extinguished.

I believe that the future of innovation among students and the future of longevity for their teachers lies in how well schools foster and embrace risk-taking, autonomy, and imagination. When schools cultivate the spark of creativity, they unleash a beacon that can light up the world.

★ ★ ★

Ashley's creative teaching epiphany is the perfect example of what we hope to do for you in this section. We hope to inspire your own journey to creative teaching *and* teaching creativity. Considering teacher effectiveness frameworks, classroom management models, and mandated teaching standards, we know that teaching often looks and sounds like a science. There is certainly some truth to that sentiment, and as we've demonstrated in this book, evidence-based practices in education are important and necessary. Still, we hope by the end of this book you'll also see teaching as an art—an art that requires innovation, imagination, risk-taking, problem solving, and just a little bit of wonder.

To start you off with some encouraging evidence, John Dewey, one of the most famous educators of all time, viewed teachers as artists, and we do, too. You'll find this metaphor interwoven in the examples in this section, and we hope this section will help you add color to your classroom canvas.

CHAPTER 16

INSPIRED BY TRAVEL

⋆Ashley

When I was in school, I thought my teachers were rich because they traveled. And they were. They were rich in stories. They were rich in worldviews. They were rich in experiences. In contrast to my grandma who has never left our small farm in East Tennessee, I reveled in hearing my teachers' travel tales, from battlefields while in history class, famous museums while in art class, and book settings while in English class.

As a child, I wanted nothing more than to be as rich as my teachers one day so that I, too, could travel! I could insert a joke here about eventually realizing the irony of teachers having lots of travel time yet little funds to do so, but in reality, my first year of teaching provided more money than I had ever experienced in my life. Inspired by my teachers, I was finally "rich" in every sense of the word.

Being inspired by travel can route you in several directions.

In case you need a push to book your summer travel plans, research has shown that travel boosts your creativity. However, don't spend your precious vacation time thinking about school. That is the whole point. When you let your mind entertain and explore things that have nothing to do with work, ideas start twinkling like the lights on the Eiffel Tower.

For example, one day while wistfully flipping through a student travel brochure, I noticed how lovely the trip descriptions sounded. With an idea in mind, I sent an email to coworkers asking for their discarded educational travel brochures and set up my lesson. I surprised my students by projecting my favorite picture from a trip to Paris, playing cliché French music, and greeting them with "Bonjour" as they walked into class. To pique their curiosity further, I displayed brochures on desks for them to flip through, their only task being to daydream.

Next, I set up the imagery writing lesson by asking them what techniques the copywriters used to help students picture themselves abroad. Then, they worked in groups to find and chart each time the writers used sensory language to allure travelers. Lastly, using their findings as a mentor text, I gave them the freedom to write about a place that is special to them in such a way that I could picture myself there.

★ ★ ★

Travel gives us the opportunity to explore the world, broaden our cultural awareness, and inspire creativity. In a literature review of "The Educational Benefits of Travel Experiences," researchers report overwhelming empirical benefits: "Personal growth, increase in life skills, and knowledge also result from independent international travel, as well as 'objectiveless' travel." Further research by Leung et al. shows us that multicultural experiences foster creativity. This research really comes as no surprise to us. In fact, you might have noticed that many of our narratives throughout the book thus far have been inspired by our own travels.

Certainly, it would be remarkable to travel with our students; however, we know firsthand the many roadblocks that can make this challenge feel impossible. While it may not be possible to take students on physical journeys to far-off places, there are many ways to open the windows of our classrooms to exploration and journey into the unknown. Interestingly, research says it might be just as effective in inspiring creativity.

As you'll learn in chapter 18, nature can provide us with space and freedom to expand our creativity. Certainly, nature itself provides many means of inspiration from beautiful colors and buzzing wildlife to wide-open spaces. As it turns out, psychological distance plays a role in this success. In "Lessons from a Faraway Land: The Effect of Spatial Distance on Creative Cognition," researchers discovered that spatial distance from a creative task (the task being perceived as far from you versus close to you) improves the creative responses of the task and problem solving. In other words, perceived spatial distance gives us the space we need to find inspiration, and nature is just one way to experience that phenomenon.

Metaphorical travel is another way to channel inspiration through psychological spatial distance. Think about it. Smaller children love packing their bags with their most prized possessions before jetting off to their backyard "desert island" or pillow fort "campsite." While we expect this from little kids, surprisingly, pretend travel can be just as exciting for older students. Let's look at an example.

Jenna

When I was a junior in college, I had a once-in-a-lifetime experience studying Shakespearean literature in Italy. During an extended spring break trip, I packed my bags and waved goodbye to my family as I boarded my first international flight. Joining a jolly group of English literature majors and professors, I traveled from western Pennsylvania to Rome to Florence to Verona to Venice to Milan, studying Shakespeare's famous plays in the locations where they took place.

To say it was a transformative experience would be an understatement. I remember so much of what I learned about Shakespearean literature during that trip, and this experience has inspired everything from my lesson planning to my design aesthetic over ten years later! Certainly, I would love to someday be the host for students on a trip of the same magnitude. However, with a little technology, I was able to provide my students with a (computer) window to my experience. Using Google's Virtual Reality Tour Creator, I created a tour that mimicked the exact trip I went on in 2007. I was even able to add specific pictures that I took on the trip into the tour creator. This virtual experience is always a hit with students.

As you noticed in the above narrative, technology can be used to facilitate curiosity through classroom-to-classroom and classroom-to-world connections.

Here are several other strategies to facilitate curiosity via metaphorical travel:

> **Mystery hangouts:** A mystery hangout is a social game played by two groups of students in different locations. Teachers from two different classrooms set up a date and time to videoconference. Skype, Google Meet, and Zoom are great options. Then, the students use a "twenty questions" format to investigate the location of the classroom. They can ask questions about the other classroom's weather, cuisine, customs, and more. Different time zones can make this tricky, but there are several asynchronous options available. Flipgrid and Padlet

are our favorite free asynchronous options. Both tech tools allow students to participate in a video or written discussion through a secure and shared platform. To get started, we suggest participating in teacher social media platforms. Facebook groups and Instagram are great places to connect with other teachers. If social media isn't your thing, Flipgrid has a program that connects classrooms all over the world.

Google Virtual Reality Tour Creator: As described above, you can create 360° street view tours for your students. For each stop, you can upload images, add narratives, or provide notes and tasks.

Virtual expeditions: Google Expeditions is a free educational tool that uses virtual reality (VR) and augmented reality (AR) to take your students on a virtual field trip. You can create your own expeditions, or you can use one of their 900 VR trips or 100 AR experiences. Consistent with our mission, we found a VR field trip exploring the New Seven Wonders of the World. With just a few clicks, we were off exploring 360° views of the Great Wall of China and Chichén Itzá.

CHAPTER 17

INSPIRED BY MINDFULNESS

The air felt too hot and sticky. My cheeks felt flushed. I was clenching my teeth.

Though I was supposed to be focusing on my next downward dog, in my head, I was thinking about feeling unprepared for the next day. I had so many essays to grade. I had so many deadlines to meet. The thoughts came pouring in. And then my yoga instructor discreetly walked over to me and told me I was holding my breath. "Focus on your breath," she reminded the class. Slow breath in. Even, steady, slow breath out. It was instant relief of the body and mind.

The next day, I was administering a test to my class of tenth graders. Looking around the room, I had an epiphany: the awkward silence, the stifling air, the tensed expressions. They were holding their breath. In that instant, I became totally aware of my own. How often was I holding my breath in all of the tough situations throughout the day? As it turns out, it was a lot . . .

Over the years, I've come to realize that "mindfulness is a path not a tool," as written in the holy grail of mindful awareness practices (MAPs) for the school setting: *Happy Teachers Change the World* by Thich Nhat Hanh and Katherine Weare. It's a path to happier teaching and learning, a path to decreased test anxiety and increased emotional awareness. It's a path to inspiration.

When our minds are clear, they are open to finding inspiration in new places, especially our own classrooms. In fact, the source cited above documents MAPs in school settings with participants ranging from elementary to college age.

Nhat Hanh and Weare's book is really more of a handbook providing educators with ideas for incorporating MAPs into their classrooms for both students and themselves. Not surprisingly, it all starts with breathing: "Teachers should master the practice of mindful breathing before they can offer it to their students. When we are able to enjoy mindful breathing, it can bring joy and help us to handle painful feelings and emotions. When teachers can do this, they naturally help their students to do the same."

Just as I learned and continue to hone, breathing awareness is a practice that starts with intentional exercises. Nhat Hanh and Weare suggest breathing statements, like coordinating the thought or saying, "I'm breathing in," with the action of breathing in. While this might seem super simple and even a bit silly, we challenge you to give it a try right now. Try three in and out breaths just like this.

How did that feel? It might have just been a subtle sensation, but with practice, these small efforts can lead us to the path of inspiration in the classroom. Let's travel down that path to Kristen Harris's classroom in Atlanta, Georgia. Kristen is an expert at using mindfulness in the classroom.

WONDER MAKER

KRISTEN HARRIS (⊡ @YOURSTRULYKRISTEN)

Why are some of my students so angry? I couldn't put my finger on it. Even though I knew many of them had challenging situations outside of school, I still felt as though their time with me, their bright and bubbly teacher, should be enough. However, who was I to judge? I had gone through a lot in my life, too, and I was using mindfulness to cope. Mindfulness . . . that's it! If it works for me, it just might work for my students as well.

At first, it felt silly asking my students to breathe with me and to dive into their emotions. It felt like quite a tall order, especially for young children. I thought they might not understand, and some didn't at first. "Why do I have to let my air out like this, Mrs. Harris?" a student asked as he giggled. Where should I even start?

"All right, friends, today I want to teach you something that Mrs. Harris loves to use every single day. Can you guess what that is?" After many wrong answers ("No, not a toothbrush," "No, not a pencil," and "No, not clothes"), I finally told them what it was. "It's . . . mindfulness!" I saw the confusion on their faces. Most of them had never heard of this concept before. I explained that practicing mindfulness helped me to regulate my emotions (or feelings) and make sense of them. We discussed, at length, what it looks like to have both appropriate and inappropriate reactions to our feelings. "Sometimes we get so mad that it's hard for us to think about what's appropriate and what's not, in the moment." They were starting to understand. They had experienced that before and could relate.

We talked about different breathing exercises like "Lion's Breath" and "In 5, Hold 5, Out 5." We discovered that redirecting our attention to our five senses would not only help us to calm down, but also to think clearly. We didn't just talk about it, though; I demonstrated and we practiced and watched child-appropriate videos on the concept. I practiced on my own, in front of them, so that they could see exactly what it's supposed to look like. Lastly, I created a "Calm Down Center" in my classroom, filled with mindful books, stress balls, our breathing activities on cards, timers, and a feelings check-in chart.

Why was I surprised when I saw academics improving and test scores increasing? Why was I surprised when my students started feeling empathy for each other or when I saw a little boy, who had gone through way more than a boy his age should have, using the breathing techniques during recess? Those students were in pre-K and so very quickly got the gist and started to reap the benefits. After three years, I went on to teaching mindfulness to third grad-ers. I was determined to change lives using the technique, and I did. It didn't just change their lives; it also positively impacted mine. If teachers showed students how to appropriately deal with their emotions and how mindful techniques can foster great suc-cess, this world would be a safer and more compassionate place.

As an educator, it's important to be mindful of the energy in your classroom. Just as Wonder Maker Kristen Harris noticed a nega-tive energy and came up with a positive solution, you, too, can be inspired by the abstract atmosphere in your teaching environment.

Be mindful and notice: Which lesson plans drain your energy and which uplift you? How can you transform the exhausting lessons into exhilarating ones? Which procedures in your classroom cause an unhealthy amount of stress on your students or yourself? What can you rethink to relieve the tension? Which activities do students diligently work on and which do they avoid? How can you adjust the work so that students concentrate instead of procrastinate? Which philosophies are you centering in your classroom? How can you transform your teacher-centered practices into student-centered, inquiry-based experiences? Which aspects of teaching fire you up and which let you down? How can you make a shift so that your passions overcompensate for your peeves?

Practicing mindfulness throughout the day means you'll be able to notice these subtle shifts in classroom energy, and if you're experiencing an inspiration block, it might be time to take a nice, slow, deep breath. In *The Art of Noticing*, author Rob Walker makes the case for practicing how to pay attention, a lost art in a distracted, hyper-connected, and productivity-obsessed world. He values the skill of noticing so much that he even challenges his graduate students with a wonder-approved assignment of "practice paying attention." His goal, he writes, is to "provoke them into thinking about what they notice, what they miss, why it matters, and how to become better, deeper, and more original observers of the world and of themselves." And isn't that precisely what every teacher wants for their students?

Noticing is at the heart of curiosity, but it also serves as the foundation of inspiration and creativity. If your goal is to inspire your students, then it only makes sense to teach them the art of paying attention.

When you're ready to inspire your students with mindfulness, here are some ideas for ways you can incorporate MAPs into your classroom:

> **Brain breaks:** When your students are ready for a break, search "brain breaks" on YouTube for fun songs or guided breathing. GoNoodle is a popular choice for brain breaks.
>
> **Meditation station:** When students are working through learning stations, make one station a MAPs station. At this station, give them a guided breathing task.
>
> **Zen zone:** Set up a corner in your room where students can go during independent work to separate themselves. You can add a sign with breathing reminders. As a bonus, yoga mats are great for floor work, and they're easy to clean!
>
> **Calming corner:** Elements in nature have a magical way of engaging the senses while calming the stress. Set up a calming corner where you have small rocks for stacking, sand for raking, and nature photography for examining.
>
> **Yoga practice poetry:** For the more advanced yogi, connect poetic analysis to yoga mindfulness. Start with a poem that embraces mindfulness themes of gratitude, self-expression, or remembrance, such as "Remember" by Joy Harjo. Then, connect the poem to yoga postures that explore these connections. If you are interested in learning how to create yoga lesson plans for the classroom, we suggest taking an educator course from Yoga Ed. They have a variety of courses for all age groups, including a Registered Children's Yoga Teacher Certificate with a Trauma-Informed Focus.

CHAPTER 18

INSPIRED BY NATURE

Ashley

In my early and naive days of teaching, I had the bright idea of creating a magical garden learning space. You see, unlike most utilitarian-designed schools, my school had an enclosed courtyard, the sole purpose of which was to provide charm, beauty, and sunshine in the middle of a cold cement structure.

I was so enamored by this slice of nature in the middle of the school that I always took the long route to the restroom just so I could pass by the courtyard along the way. As I walked by day after day, I couldn't help but wonder why no one ever used this enchanting space. To start, the doors leading to the fully enclosed space were locked. This meant that any teacher who wanted to take their lesson outdoors had to request a key. This extra step created just enough friction to deter teachers who had a fleeting idea to surprise their students with outdoor learning time. Secondly, the courtyard had ledges to sit on, but no tables, which made it challenging to think past the typical desk setting teachers had in their comfortable classrooms.

With these sticking points in mind, I formed an ambitious plan to turn a lonely unused courtyard into a lively outdoor classroom. I worked with the office closest to the courtyard for a key solution, I organized a flower planting day with my student craft club, and I enlisted the help of our enthusiastic student council to generate funds for patio tables. But just as my vision for a magical garden classroom started to flow freely, it hit a clog. Someone with a much more experienced artistic eye than I became privy to our plans and shut us down. It turns out the professionally designed courtyard could not be tainted by patio tables that did not align with its originally intended design aesthetic. And so that was the end of that, or so I thought.

One lovely spring day as I walked past the lush courtyard expecting to see it deserted as always, I noticed it wasn't empty after all! Much to my surprise, right in the middle of the perfectly designed pavers sat an incongruous, dingy, smelly, old . . . toilet. I stood there in astonishment taking in the absurd sight and clapped my hands over my face to hold in my laughter. The prankster who snuck the toilet into the school had a sense of humor, that's for sure! When I composed myself, I got the courtyard key and held all of my classes in the courtyard that day. How could I not? For starters, I now had a throne to teach from, but most importantly, this was a teachable moment!

★ ★ ★

When you try to create something beautiful in life, there will always be obstacles. Some fresh newbie might jump in and want to disturb what you have created. Some prankster might plop a toilet right down in the middle of your preservation. In short, someone will inevitably poo-poo on your plans. It's up to you to focus on the things you can control, make sure your "why" is in the right place, and then flush the other stuff down the drain.

Like most things in life, compromise is usually the answer. Another outdoor classroom enthusiast on my team wrote a grant and was awarded funds to purchase a class set of portable table tops. These makeshift desks are stored in a closet beside the courtyard, and now any teacher who wants to create a flexible outdoor classroom in the aesthetically preserved courtyard has the means to do so. One of a teacher's simple pleasures in school life is seeing the delight on students' faces when they say, "Let's go outside and learn today!" Pure joy sparked by a sense of freedom outside confining classroom walls!

In the book *Joyful,* Ingrid Fetell Lee explores why nature sparks joy in our lives. She describes nature as "evok[ing] a response that is simultaneously joyful and calming ('emotionally positive' and 'low arousing' in psychologists' terms)." She goes on to beautifully describe scenic senses and how we often feel most alive when surrounded by life.

In addition to that fun fresh-air feeling, the brain benefits of learning outdoors are also rooted in research. For starters, varying study location improves retention. In the *New York Times* article "Forget What You Know About Good Study Habits," Benedict Carey breaks down a classic 1978 experiment in which "psychologists found that college students who studied a list of forty vocabulary words in two different rooms—one windowless and cluttered, the other modern with a view on a courtyard—did far better on a test than students who studied the words twice in the same room. Later studies have confirmed the finding, for a variety of topics." Now, this particular study didn't focus on outdoor study benefits, but if you can't find a place to roam within the school, then an outdoor area could be perfect for improving retention by moving about.

A second brain benefit to learning outdoors is that nature increases brain function. In the article "How Nature Can Make You Kinder, Happier, and More Creative," Jill Suttie summarizes research on how nature affects the brain with evidence that the outdoors can increase attention, creativity, and brain function. One study she cites from *Psychological Science* found that the impact of nature on attention restoration is what accounted for improved scores on cognitive tests for the study participants. So whether you are looking for more creativity or better focus, nature is the answer.

Third, and fitting for this chapter, open air promotes an open mind and freedom of expression. A fascinating study in the *Journal of Consumer Research* reveals that ceiling height confines our thinking. However, if you can't raise the roof in your room, take a note from Melissa Burkley writing for *Psychology Today*: "High ceilings unconsciously activate thoughts of freedom, which causes the brain to think in the abstract and to consider how things are related and integrated. [Go outside because] nature, of course, has no ceiling." Using this information to turn poetic metaphors into a literal application, wide-open spaces may prime brains for out-of-the-box thinking, and bright skies may prompt brainstormers to shoot for the stars! So as you consider how to tangibly provide inspirational activities for your students, ponder how a little sunshine could spark creative thinking in the world outside your room.

Here's some inspiration for learning outdoors:

- **Memory motion:** Take a walk in tandem, with partners quizzing each other on a memorization task.
- **Podcast paths:** When students are listening to a podcast for class, take advantage of the portable nature of podcast devices and go on a listening and learning stroll.
- **Rustic reading:** Consider chunking extended reading time by changing up chapter locations.
- **Invigorating interdisciplinary:** Often, cross-curricular classes don't collaborate because there simply isn't enough space, but the great outdoors remedies this!

- **Picnic PBL:** Projects can be messy. Ponder how your next project may be better suited for an outdoor space.
- **Literature landscapes:** Enhance and evaluate a book's setting by reenacting important sections outdoors.
- **Yard yoga:** Stretch minds and bodies with pedagogical poses outside.
- **Grassy gallery walk:** The gallery walk strategy is great for movement, so take advantage of extra space outside your classroom walls.
- **Standardized sidewalk:** Make test prep more fun by taping individual questions outdoors. Students take a stroll, keep records of answers, then self-check on the second loop.
- **Flora and formative assessment:** Think of ways of turning your go-to formative assessment strategies into outdoor activities. Instead of doing a mini quiz indoors, perhaps students can toss pebbles into A, B, C, or D spots outside.
- **Cool breeze composition:** Oftentimes students are inspired to write better outdoors. Consider taking notebooks or computers outside for writing time.
- **Lawn languages:** Often considered a dry topic, grammar can come alive in an outdoor setting. For example, have students create human compound and complex sentences in a big open area outdoors where they can move around freely to find their syntax matches.
- **Fresh air, fresh ideas:** The confines of the classroom can make brainstorming for creative or structured writing a challenge. Take students outdoors for a brainstorming session.
- **Scenic scavenging:** Send your students on a nature scavenger hunt. You can provide them with a list of items. Use these items to work on concepts like imagery or symbolism.
- **Socratic senses:** Open up your Socratic seminar to the great outdoors so students can open their minds during this

student-led discussion. After your seminar, ask students to reflect on how the setting influenced the discussion. You may find that it's just what students needed to feel more inquisitive and empowered.

- **Sunny stations:** We love learning stations, especially when we can take them outside. Your school just might have the perfect space if you practice the art of noticing on your walk to the parking lot. You'll soon see that tree, sidewalk, or picnic table as a new spot for a station!

- **Courtyard collaboration:** Consider changing the scenery for small-group work and giving students the chance to space out and collaborate. Then, bring students back to a whole-group setting to see how the freedom of nature energized their discussions.

CHAPTER 19

INSPIRED BY STUDENTS

According to Dr. George Land in his talk for TEDxTucson, a creativity assessment originally designed for NASA was administered to sixteen hundred US children. Their results? An incredible ninety-eight percent of four- to five-year-olds scored in the assessment's so-called "genius zone." But just five years later, when the test was given to the same children, their results dropped to thirty percent, only to plummet to twelve percent after another five years. For reference, a mere two percent of adults score in the high creativity category on this same assessment.

Dr. Land makes sense of these results by highlighting the difference between creative or divergent thinking that explores possibilities and convergent thinking that narrows down information to a "correct" answer. While the statistics are discouraging, he offers a simple suggestion of exercising our divergent thinking muscles. Ask your five-year-old for twenty-five suggestions on how to improve a table fork, he proposes, and you'll be on your way to more imaginative thinking.

But you don't need to have children (or even table forks) of your own to sharpen your creative thinking skills. After all, you have a classroom full of students who, no offense, just might be more creative than you. Take advantage of this opportunity and embrace your students' divergent thinking. Make time for brainstorming, experimentation, inquiry, and play, and then watch what your students do when freed from the chains of convergent thinking. Be observant and take note of how you can apply that same sense of exploration to your lessons.

There's something even more simple and transformative that you can do with the little "creative geniuses" in your classroom: Ask them for ideas. Invite their feedback. Embrace their questions. Listen to their seemingly ridiculous chatter. And, when you can, find a way to take them up on their daydreams and wild ideas.

When Abby's students asked, "Can we go on a field trip to Alaska?" during their *Into the Wild* unit, she gave them a tour of Chris McCandless's journey with interactive 360° views, thanks to Google Maps and Google Earth. When she asked her students what they wanted to learn before they graduated and they semi-sarcastically replied, "How to make more money," she planned a unit on "real-life persuasion," complete with lessons on social media marketing. And when she overheard her students joking about how their conjoined desks made it look like they were speed dating each other, she imagined and executed a "speed debating" lesson for the very next day.

When Ashley realized her students constantly had earbuds attached to their ears, she capitalized by introducing them to podcasts. Several fully engaged podcast lessons later, what once was a symbol of distraction now holds the possibility of a free library of audio stories, informational texts, memoirs, and more. When she noticed the mini Play-Doh containers were the first to go out of her prize bucket, she created a lesson so that all her students could "play" by building microcosms using dough, symbols, and textual evidence from *Lord of the Flies*.

When Staci heard some of her seniors talking about *How to Get Away with Murder*, she designed an assignment for their *Macbeth* unit in which students created *Lady Macbeth's Handbook on How to Get Away with Murder*. When her freshmen talked about *Shark Tank*, she created a lesson all about ethos, logos, and pathos, complete with a handout with a totally real shark bite missing from the corner. When she found a text generator online for students to create fake conversations between characters, the students actually suggested just using their own phones and changing the contact names in their threads and on Snapchat.

When Jenna overheard her students talking about *The Bachelor*, she created a poetry competition complete with handing out a red, red rose to the winner. When she saw a student intricately folding a note in class, she added an origami symbolism challenge to her next unit. When she noticed her students sharing pictures of their prom dresses, she created a paper doll dress-up lesson to teach her students about Victorian-era fashion while reading *The Importance of Being Earnest*.

It can be even simpler. Before your unit, ask your students what they know and what they want to learn. In the middle of your unit, talk to them about their ideas. Consider their examples, connections, and questions and how you can turn them into lessons. At the end of your unit, ask them what helped them learn, what they liked, and what they wish you'd have done. Sure, you'll get the occasional "don't assign the essay" response, but you'll also find nuggets of inspiration for your next unit or the following year. Follow those what-ifs and wild ideas, and you'll be surprised where they take you. If you follow your students' lead, you'll find all the inspiration you need.

CHAPTER 20

INSPIRED BY ART

Staci

When I lived alone, my friends would always pick on me because I had no decorations in my house. I invested no money into wall art or decorative items for around the house, whereas with my classroom, I'm quite the opposite.

It wasn't until I moved in with my best friend and colleague Anna that I realized maybe, just maybe, I should create a happy space at home, too, filled with pieces that bring me joy and peace. On a shopping trip to HomeGoods, I found a beautifully framed piece of art with the quote "Let joy be your compass."

Something about those words resonated with me. If you recall, I pursued teaching because it brought me joy whereas a career in a cubicle would not have done the same. That quote has become one I often refer to when I make decisions, including one decision after our live Keeping the Wonder Workshop in Lexington. After the workshop, I was inspired yet again by the energy from the one-hundred-plus educators who joined us. I was fueled with joy, and what did my compass inspire me to do? Get a tattoo, of course! My friend Anna and I found a local tattoo shop, and on my right forearm is the dainty "Let joy be your compass" quote. While it now has a new, even more profound sentimental meaning to me as I connect it to my experiences with Keeping the Wonder, I often still look at the art that now hangs in my bedroom.

Like Staci, have you ever looked at a piece of artwork and wondered why? Why did the artist choose that color? Why is the author telling a story with this piece? Why is this piece striking a chord for me?

That's what art does for us. It provides a visual stimulus to draw out our whys, something adulthood answers with work, stress, and plans. We already know children are particularly good at asking why. Just ask any kindergarten teacher! *Why is the sky blue? Why can't I run down the hall? Why is the dog in the story brown?*

This is something Philip Yenawine, author of *Visual Thinking Strategies: Using Art to Deepen Learning Across School Disciplines*, recognized when he was running the education program at the Museum of Modern Art (MOMA) in New York. At first, he was completely overwhelmed with the thought of answering all of his patrons' whys; however, he soon realized the problem. In his words, "After a great deal of thought—while digesting developmental research and theory by cognitive psychologist Abigail Housen and others—we realized the problem. What MOMA visitors really needed . . . [was] not answers, but the permission to be puzzled and think."

Children don't need permission to ask why. But as Yenawine realized, adults do. Right now, we're giving you permission to ask why. In fact, we're encouraging you. Let's do a simple practice to prime your inspiration. Look at the illustration. Then, take a minute, and jot down your whys. Get as creative as you can!

Were you able to come up with five whys? Ten whys? Twenty? As you can see, wonderings can be prompted. In fact, Karen Morse, writing for the National Association for Gifted Children, suggests prompting "wonderings" by asking children open-ended questions about their artistic observations. These observations can take place in nature, in a museum, or in a picture book. Here are some examples:

- What do you think it would be like if everything in the world was the color of this leaf?
- What do you think the animal in that painting is thinking?
- Why do you think the girl is wearing that color?

What we're really doing for children by encouraging wonderings is teaching them what Yenawine calls visual thinking strategies (VTS). The point is to teach students strategies rather than give answers.

The Museum of Fine Arts, Houston, suggests a four-step approach that is characteristic of the guides you'll find on many museum websites: look, describe, think, and connect. We chose this particular approach because we like how well it can be adapted to classroom contexts.

- **Look:** As we discussed in Curiosity, ask, "What did you notice?" We also love the idea of giving a thirty-second looking period, followed by a challenge to recall what details students can recall without the image in front of them.
- **Describe:** This step is a superficial overview from the looking experience, paying attention to colors, images, textures, and shapes.
- **Think:** Now it's time to practice visual literacy to assign meaning to the work. Mood is an important concept to think about, and perhaps do a little research about the artist and time period to gather context.
- **Connect:** Comparing and contrasting to other forms of art and stimulating memories are good ways to connect the piece to other works and situations.

Combining VTS with art creation brings this inspiration endeavor full circle. For good reason, research overwhelmingly tells us that visualizing and creating art in the classroom benefits abstract thinking, language development, social and emotional skills, problem solving, creative thinking, class participation, relaxation, fine motor skills, confidence, and self-expression.

Considering all of these benefits, we have a final why for you: Why would we limit artwork to the art classroom? LaQuisha Hall, a 2018 Maryland Teacher of the Year finalist, believes we shouldn't.

An expert in integrating art in her classroom through visual notes, LaQuisha shares her inspiration for using art in her ninth-grade ELA classroom.

WONDER MAKER

LAQUISHA HALL (⊙ @MRSHALLSCHOLARS)

Educator Robert John Meehan said, "Don't struggle to be a better teacher than everybody else. Simply be a better teacher than you ever thought you could be."

I began preparing for my scholars in early April 2018. I knew that I wanted to push myself as an educator to offer more variety and creative opportunities. I will not only report that my plan worked, but it exceeded my expectations. I spent months conveying the need of high-interest, culturally diverse books for my scholars to my social media community. To my surprise, all of the books I requested were purchased by generous donors. I selected four diverse titles and secured more than two hundred books total. These books would change the trajectory of reading for the freshmen and juniors I was preparing to teach.

I individually surveyed my scholars three times that school year. At the very start of school, most of them shared through frowning faces that they abhorred reading prior to high school, and the last book they could remember reading was the text required in the fourth quarter of eighth grade. Many also shared that they did not have any books of their own nor did they have a favorite book, author, or series. The findings of my survey disturbed me greatly. Here they were sitting in my classroom looking at me like, "What are you going to do differently than we have done before?"

I understood that whatever reading and writing measures I modeled and whatever lessons I created, they had to be extraordinary and unlike any prior experiences they (and I) had before.

I wanted to expose my new scholars to my new books. I was tremendously excited for them to read the diverse books I had collected and I knew that if I could just hook them in, they would not mind reading them. But again, their prior experiences with books would probably have caused them to shut down at the sight of a book. I opened "Starbooks Café" in my classroom. I showed up to class with the books intricately displayed on their café tables (desks) with decorations to resemble a coffee shop. I stood at the door and greeted them in all black, wearing a green apron and a name tag with a large Starbooks logo that read "Mrs. Hall, Bookrista." Initially, my scholars looked at me with shock, especially since I did this during the second week of school.

Soon, however, my scholars not only bought in to Starbooks Café, they loved it! Some of them had the opportunity to wear a green apron, too, as they were "hired" to help me distribute hot chocolate and donuts while their peers browsed the variety of books. I could hear some of them saying in their small groups, "I want to read this one because this sounds like Baltimore!" or "I like this cover! This looks new!" My heart was overwhelmed as I knew I had grabbed them.

The next challenge was to change their reading habits. While many of them loved their self-selected book, they did not possess the reading stamina to sit and read. Beginning the day after our first Starbooks Café, I challenged them to read for the first fifteen to twenty minutes of class. The key: not only did I read with them, but I read *their* books with them. Scholars who were reading the same book would ask me questions about my thoughts afterward or say statements like, "Mrs. Hall, wait until you read page 102!" Something I did not teach them was not to share spoilers, but I appreciated being able to share this time and space with them.

My scholars went from fidgeting and looking out the window to emphatically requesting five more minutes when I would call their reading time to a close. All of this transpired in the first quarter of the school year.

Finally, another opportunity I offered my scholars was a creative outlet. I immersed myself in the study of visual notes—what it was, the research behind it, and its academic benefits. As an artist and educator, I have always been dedicated to finding ways to tap in to all of the learning styles of my variety of scholars. As a result of my research and personal reading of the diverse books I piled up in my classroom, I began to create one-pagers that visually and linguistically gave a summation of key ideas and my learning from each text I read. After enjoying and participating in this creative process myself, I introduced this to my scholars and they took off! My scholars created the most beautiful masterpieces connecting books to art and writing.

I repeated the Starbooks Café, revealing more books to them over the course of the school year and allowing them to choose what they read. They participated in literature circles and discussed the books they shared in common with their peers. They created visual presentations of their favorite texts through visual notes and one-pagers. I could hear conversations like, "Girl, you have to read this book next! It's so good!" and "Man, this book is thick, but it doesn't feel like it because it keeps you reading!" And of course, my favorite line: "Mrs. Hall, can I take this book home? I promise to bring it back tomorrow!"

The results of this creative and artistic innovation in my classroom were amazing to me and I wished I had started doing these activities sooner in my career. I started to receive messages from former scholars, like "You didn't do all of that for us, Mrs. Hall!" and "Can I come to your room after lunch and borrow that book?"

A parent contacted me and shared that he had no idea how I got his child to read at home, and he was shocked. He thanked me and assured me that his child would promptly return the book when finished. I was too proud not to tell him that his child and all of his peers received a copy to keep, beginning their own home libraries. He was thrilled and promised his continued support of all my efforts as an educator.

I am not sharing this with you to brag. My scholars are just like all scholars across the country: seeking the investment of time, love, and resources from those they should be able to look up to. I am no different than any other educator in our country. I share with educators because I want them to boldly use their creativity as a professional to create a Starbooks Café and display of visual notes. I want parents to ask their young learners what books they are bringing home, for what class, and which teacher gave it to them. I want the community to continue not only to support our teachers and schools, but support district leaders as they implement equitable policies and practices that benefit our scholars.

Ask our leaders questions before lashing out in anger to understand the why in the implemented policies. Without the support of all parties who encounter our youth, the important work that must be done will not be solidified. We need you, the reader of this book, the woman sitting at the bus stop, the man looking out the window as our scholars pass their home to go to school . . . we need you ALL to support by voting in all elections, by not believing everything you hear in the media, by not saying you are here to help our youth and then go to a friend and discuss how "terrible these kids are." If you do encounter negativity, suggest to that person that they can help make our schools better by applying to become an educator. If you are going to talk about it, be about it—be about the work of ensuring a future of triumph for all young scholars who desire to express themselves creatively.

LaQuisha's wise words remind us that we don't need to be da Vinci to teach with art, and your students don't have to either. We encourage you to look at art, or even academics, in a playful, nontraditional way to stimulate the senses and ultimately lead to inquiry and inspiration. In his book *The Art of Noticing*, Rob Walker tells the story of Museum Hack, a company that, according to its website, offers "renegade, small-group tours for people who *think* they don't like museums." Their out-of-the-ordinary, engaging tours promise unique, clever, and playful experiences designed to make attendees rethink art and museums.

Walker also mentions one kind of creative "noticing game" that works for art, books, or any other tangible items: "Buy, Burn, or Steal." While it's nontraditional, this kind of game is a brilliant way to trick museumgoers into noticing the art, and it certainly stirs up lively arguments about what is worthy of a frame and what is better suited for some matches and kindling.

As a curious "tour guide," you can use this same kind of clever reimagining to inspire your students and trick them into learning. Maybe this means posing a "Use, Lose, or Abuse" game for students to playfully approach their vocabulary lists or making a game out of the mundane. Whatever you do, the point is simple: Take a traditionally uninspiring assignment or experience, and find a new way to notice it. Flip it on its head, break the rules, and give your students a new lens for their divergent thinking.

Here are some other ways you and your students can tap into your artistic side:

Reading art closely: One of our Wonder Makers, Vennieta Grant, created a powerful and stunning lesson using the art of Kadir Nelson that expertly demonstrates how close reading of art can not only build confidence with striving readers but also lead to even deeper analysis than texts allow.

Posting several pieces of art by Nelson into a virtual gallery, she first prompted students just to look at the art and jot down the visual facts of what they saw (first "read"). Next, she had them take a second look at the artwork with a prompt to wonder. "I wonder why . . . " "I'm puzzled by . . . " "If I could interview the artist, I would ask . . . " "How would it be different if . . . " etc. (second "read"). Lastly, she instructed students to make connections by selecting two of their favorite paintings in the gallery, listing several things they have in common (third "read").

After closely reading the art, she was then able to ask critical thinking questions like "What did the artist want to communicate with this piece, and what in the image proves this?" When students are successful with this deep level of analysis, they will be much more confident when your questions replace the "artist" with "author."

Building art models: One day during a poetry lesson, Jenna was inspired to pull out the Play-Doh for a close-reading remake. Her class was reading "Ozymandias," a poem inspired by a discovery of part of Ramesses II's statue. She asked her students to close read the poem independently and then attempt to create a Play-Doh sculpture of the poet's description of the artifact. Her classroom became an art gallery of sculptures, and students helped each other interpret the poem to "improve" their sculptures.

Processing current events: As the saying goes, a picture is worth a thousand words, and oftentimes when no words seem good enough, art can express the words that fail us. Rather than shying away from current events for fear of saying something wrong, let art do the talking. In the fast-paced world of social media, artists emerge to express themes of unity, justice, and humanity. Consider displaying poignant works of art the day after a difficult event and asking students to reflect with these prompts: "What did you see?" "How did it make you feel?" "What do you wonder?" This simple strategy can help students process jarring current events, as well as joyful ones!

For example, after Amanda Gorman's inauguration poetry reading, Ashley used two artistic depictions of the inspirational poet for a reflective mini-lesson. Following the initial prompts mentioned above, she asked, "How did artist one interpret the tone of Gorman's poem, and how do you know?" "How does artist one compare to artist two, and which elements of the art show you this?" Then lastly, "Which art speaks to you the most and why?" This quick art lesson celebrated an incredible poet, acknowledged an important current event, and allowed for an insightful class discussion.

Forming word-art summaries: Thinking of a way to make time period introductions more engaging, Ashley decided to have her students summarize what they learned from their reading into word-art summaries. First, they read about the time period silently. Next, they did a second read, highlighting the parts they thought were most important to understanding the culture and history of the time period. Then they got into groups to discuss their highlighted points and come to a consensus. Lastly, they were tasked with summarizing their findings into word art. For example, the "R" in "Renaissance" could be formed by a paintbrush, gold coin, and royal scepter to represent the funding dynamic of this time period. Word-art summaries work with informational text, character names, book titles, historical figures, and more!

Creating concrete poetry: When Staci and her students read *Long Way Down* by Jason Reynolds, the students quickly realized how poetry can be transformed from just words on a page to artistic expressions. Reynolds incorporates concrete poetry into his work, so the students had a chance to create their own examples and also add color, backgrounds, and images. One creative student wrote a poem about confusion that students face, and his poem was written in the shape of a question mark. This unit also tied nicely into blackout poetry, which is another example of how visual art and poetry can be combined.

Making musical connections: Music is an art form, and it provides a great way to inspire students to make connections. In fact, the VTS outlined from the Museum of Fine Arts, Houston, can easily be adapted for listening—just switch out "look" for "listen." Using the Listen, Describe, Think, and Connect model, Jenna created a series of stations for students to analyze their favorite song to make a broader connection to poetry. She modeled the strategy as a class first, by playing the song "While My Guitar Gently Weeps" by the Beatles. Next, students described what they heard and thought about the meaning. Finally, to bring in a visual element, she showed the painting *The Old Guitarist* by Pablo Picasso, so students could compare and contrast mood and meaning.

Imagining imagery: When she is teaching a text rich with imagery and other forms of figurative language, Abby loves to challenge her students to visually represent the excerpt. She purposefully keeps instructions vague and the risks low so that students have the freedom to interpret this assignment in different ways. After students create their visual representations, she facilitates a whole-class discussion, asking students to compare their renderings and analyze how word choice affects tone and mood.

Whether you are asking your students to analyze the art of Kadir Nelson or the poetry of Jason Reynolds, bringing art into the classroom can breathe new life into your curriculum. Better yet, art can inspire your students and help them understand the world around them.

CHAPTER 21

INSPIRED BY PERSPECTIVE

Often, we do not feel inspired because we are stuck in the same routines and mentally fatigued by the daily demands of teaching and life. Even if we want to think creatively, it doesn't come naturally when our brain is preoccupied or blinded by doing what it's always done. Students experience this as well. The same old routines can leave them feeling just as uninspired. As we've demonstrated throughout this book, there are so many strategies that we can use to provide a new perspective to a typical school day.

Sparking surprise, creating curiosity, and forging freedom are endeavors that inspire wonder. The same can be said for creativity. In fact, as reported by Eyal Doron and Ellen Galinksy in their respective research, school-aged children inspired by new perspectives exhibit more empathy, cognitive flexibility, and creativity. Since we've already covered these strategies for students, let's focus on you.

Sometimes teachers need a new perspective for inspiration as well.

Jenna

Fresh out of an inspiring student teaching experience, I couldn't wait to pour my creative energy into lesson planning. And then, the first day in my own classroom hit me with a ton of standardized test prep, classroom management considerations, record-keeping responsibilities, school-day duties, and so much more. I was so overwhelmed with all of the new teacher struggles that I lost a lot of my inspiration.

I pretty quickly fell into the textbook-provided study guide trap. To manage the hecticness of the everyday, my lessons looked a lot like "review questions from the study guide." I lost my lesson-planning mojo.

To get it back, I needed a new lens to think about lesson planning, so I went back to my favorite class in college: Literary Theory. Literary Theory is one of the most notorious classes for English majors because of its philosophical nature. However, at its core, literary theory is really just different perspectives of interpreting text.

Using these theories as lenses for lesson planning, I was inspired to see new perspectives for my own units. I enjoyed this process so much that I dedicated my dissertation to using new perspectives, or lenses, to inspire the lesson planning process. Now, when creating a new curriculum, I start with perspectives related to the objectives of the unit. Then, I choose works that relate to those perspectives. This is a great way to open windows to new perspectives in the classroom and inspire me to seek out literature related to diverse voices and experiences.

According to *An Educator's Guide to Promoting Perspective Taking Skills in the Classroom*, "perspective taking is a very broad psychological term that captures a skill set your students will use to explore their world, to understand and to connect with their peers and families, and to improve upon their academic performance." This definition applies to educators, as well, so let's try it this way: "Perspective taking is a very broad psychological term that captures a skill set [you] will use to explore [the] world, to understand and to connect with [your students,] peers, and families, and to improve upon [your own teaching] performance." I argue these substitutions do not change the meaning.

✶ ✶ ✶

To find inspiration in perspective-taking, think about all of the perspectives that are valuable to your content. Sometimes this might mean looking for underserved voices and finding a way to frame an activity to serve them. Other times, it might mean putting yourself in your student's desk to view your lesson from their point of view.

Inspiration comes from new perspectives.

To give you a head start, we're ending this chapter with a series of what-ifs and questions designed to shift your thinking enough to spark an idea. These questions were partially inspired by some of Abby's late-night, last-minute, or on-the-spot lessons (you know, the ones that ended up being even better than some of her meticulously detailed plans) and a clever deck of cards created by two musicians.

Called Oblique Strategies, these cards were the brainchild of musician Brian Eno and composer Peter Schmidt. According to an article on BrainPickings.org, the two created a deck of cards designed to jump-start creativity in the recording studio. Some cards contain reminders like "Take a break" or sage advice like "If a thing can be said, it can be said simply," while others challenge the artists to "Abandon normal instruments" or "Tape [their] mouth." Some encourage a fresh perspective, like "Use non-musicians" or "Shut the front door and listen from outside," while others are just plain weird: "Imagine the music as a moving chain or caterpillar." What they all have in common is a disruption, a pause, and time to reflect. And as abstract as some of the cards may be, they've been used to create music by David Bowie, Coldplay, and others, according to the *Guardian*. So, depending on your musical tastes, they work!

To get you thinking on how you can translate this kind of inspiration to your teaching practices, here are a few challenges and questions to help you reflect. Remember, the purpose of this exercise is to help you think divergently and explore your options. Not every question will spark a genius idea. In fact, most won't, but if you flex your creative thinking muscles, you'll learn to disrupt your routines and challenge your pedagogy. In other words, you'll learn to inspire yourself.

THE WHAT-IFS

What if the internet went down and you had no technology? Or the flip side, depending on what's scarier for you: What if you had no paper? Even more challenging: What if you had no resources at all?

What if you had only ten minutes to plan? Surely you've experienced the joy of a spontaneous, last-minute plan that ended up being better than the lesson you agonized over for hours. What if you could recreate this? Set a timer for ten minutes and see what you can dream up.

What if you flipped the hard work on the students? Skim our Freedom section in search of ways to switch your lesson so that it's student-centered. The mere act of flipping the workload on students will often require you to think in a more innovative way.

What if you taught this lesson in the simplest way possible? What does that look like? It might not be flashy, but it could be effective. Don't limit yourself by overthinking and overplanning.

What if you used someone else's plans? Maybe now is not the time for creative genius. Maybe you can free up some brain space, use another teacher's lesson, and reflect.

IN A PERFECT WORLD . . .

If standardized testing, standards, and data didn't exist, how would you teach this? For once, don't let "reality" shut down your divergent thinking. Give yourself permission to dream of that "perfect world." Once you have ideas, you can always find a way to weave the standards back in.

If you had all the time in the world, how would you teach this? Allow yourself to pursue this, and then think of a plan B. And if you have no time, save your ideas for next year! Abby loves creating "Just an Idea" Google Docs so she has inspiration to return to the following year.

If you knew your idea wouldn't fail, how would you teach this? Then take the risk! Do it before you feel ready, because you might never feel prepared! The worst-case scenario is actually the best-case scenario, because even if it totally flops, you'll learn from it.

OTHER PERSPECTIVES . . .

How might [a coach, your favorite teacher, a business executive, an artist, a comedian, your grandma, etc.] teach this lesson? Fill in the blank and visualize what this lesson might look like from a different perspective. Think from a few different lenses, and then combine the best bits and pieces to form a well-rounded, out-of-the-box lesson plan.

What simile, metaphor, symbol, or analogy best represents this lesson? For a second, stop staring at the standards and start thinking about symbolism. Challenge yourself to find three different ways to represent your content, and then pick the idea that inspires you the most. Here's an example for a lesson on thesis statements: A thesis statement is like 1) a road map to your essay, 2) a clear and concise tweet, or 3) a tour guide on a hike.

Think like a student and answer the burning question: Why do I need to learn this? Really answer it. Focus on the most important, immediate uses of the skill or content, and find a creative way to increase buy-in from your students.

Take a break and expose yourself to new information or ideas. Listen to a podcast, read a book, talk to a friend, or even turn on the TV. Creativity is all about connections, so if you're not exposing your brain to anything new, you'll run on teacher autopilot, stuck in your routines.

For our final Wonder Maker journey, we're traveling to Vennieta Grant's classroom at Lynwood Unified School District in California. Vennieta has been with us from the beginning of Keeping the Wonder, so it's only fitting that her vignette appears at the end of this book. After attending our workshop at the enchanting Hammond Castle in Gloucester, Massachusetts, Vennieta dusted off her workshop Spellnotes. Capitalizing on her own magic, Vennieta shows us how a tiny drop of wonder from one of our workshops can transform into an enchanting lesson.

WONDER MAKER

VENNIETA GRANT (@LOVETEACHREPEAT)

At the start of the year, my goal was to build my students' arsenal, or cognitive thinking toolkit, by modeling and routinely giving them ample opportunities to analyze a vast array of both literary and informational text. Although they seemed to be gaining confidence utilizing various reading and analytical strategies to understand the theme of a given text, many of my students would often shy away from and, for some, totally opt out of the writing portions of my lessons.

It didn't matter how many sentence frames I offered, prewriting activities I scaffolded, or carefully worded rubrics I provided; they were struggling to see the benefit and, most importantly, lacked a sense of connectedness and ownership over their writing. I didn't know how, but I knew that I was determined to find a new strategy to help them develop as writers.

Who would have thought that I would find the answer to my teaching quandary in an enchanted castle, surrounded by a community of magical educators? While attending the Keeping the Wonder Workshop, I participated in a session where Staci Lamb introduced me to a new strategy, known as "Reading like a Writer." While listening to Staci present, I had an epiphany: my students did not *see* themselves as writers. Although they were able to utilize reading and annotation strategies to identify aspects of an author's craft, they struggled to develop a rationale for the intentionality behind the choices that a writer makes to develop a unique writing aesthetic. As I flew home, I toyed with ways to modify and adapt the strategy for them.

This particular lesson started with a proclamation of sorts, in which I referred to every student as a writer. For the students who disagreed, we quickly discussed the definition of the term "writer," and even Harold, one of the most resistant, had to agree that he had successfully penned a few constructed responses in his lifetime. As a class, we watched two television commercials, one from a well-known insurance company full of satire, puns, and other easy-to-identify humorous elements. In contrast, the second video had a somber tone and featured a famous NBA player discussing how he overcame life's adversity.

While watching each video, students critiqued their "colleagues" (the writer/director of each video) and documented their responses on the Reading like a Writer handout. Students shared their observations and analysis with a partner, and we charted our collective responses. I immediately began to see my students' understanding shift. They shared their responses regarding the way each commercial made them feel and how their "colleagues" were able to elicit such feelings and reactions.

When they returned to class after a break, they were surprised to find a personalized nameplate with "Reader" written on one side and "Writer" on the reverse, along with a vignette from Sandra Cisneros's *The House on Mango Street.* For the first "chunk" of the vignette, I performed an animated think aloud in which I used alternate voices to represent my role and perspective of both a reader and a writer. The students then worked with a partner to finish analyzing the vignette, flipping their nameplates to indicate which role they were assuming.

The best part of the lesson was witnessing my students role-play conversations between Sandra Cisneros and her readers. This activity served as an excellent tool for assessing their understanding of the author's craft, and helped to solidify this concept for some of my students who needed the skill and concept presented in an alternate modality. At the conclusion of this lesson, they were able to independently write vignettes, mimicking the nuances of Cisneros's craft and style as an author. As the year progressed, they were able to explain the intentionality of their own writing choices, style, and purpose.

As a result of this strategy, my class developed a keen awareness of an author's craft and ultimately reframed the way they see themselves as writers and consumers of literature.

As you can tell, Vennieta is a phenomenal educator, and one piece of her power lies in her ability to combine the elements of wonder in one beautifully alluring lesson:

- She dazzled her students with **surprise** nametags as a flash-bulb prop.
- She primed her students' **curiosity** with a video inference challenge.
- She granted them **freedom** to share their observations openly and honestly.
- She encouraged **inspiration** through the use of a mentor text.

By mixing your own powers with the elements of wonder in this book, you can create your own wonder-filled lessons. To do just that, following the conclusion we leave with you a wonder kit, filled with the ingredients from this book to make learning magical. When you're ready to create your own magic, we hope you'll flip to the following pages to find an organized list of all of the ideas from this book.

CONCLUSION

mag·ic
/ˈmajik/
noun: the power of apparently influencing the course
of events by using mysterious or supernatural forces.

Teachers are magic.

Casting a spell, a teacher empowers a shy and silent student to find their voice. With cunning trickery, a teacher disguises learning as a game. Captivating with care, a teacher creates a classroom of empathy and equity. With a sleight of hand, a teacher transforms the classroom into a whimsical world of wonder and learning.

Spinning an illusion of fantasy, a teacher ferries the classroom to faraway places. With the bewitchment of a book, a teacher transports their students to a new world of words. Giving sage advice, a teacher mentors their students in their own magic-making. With a little hocus-pocus, a teacher designs an irresistible learning experience that transcends a mere lesson. Sprinkling some glamour, a teacher delights and amazes.

With the help of a little wonder, a teacher discovers the antidote for lethargy, boredom, and apathy. By being an educator, you directly influence the course of events in the lives of children. You have the power to lead, inspire, and transform. You are magical. You are a wonder maker. We want you to realize the magic within yourself and feel empowered by your talents.

With this book, we hope that we have inspired you to keep the wonder for your students, as well as yourself. Remember, in addition to surprise, curiosity, freedom, and inspiration, the most important element in creating wonder is YOU.

WONDER KIT

SURPRISE

CURIOSITY

FREEDOM

INSPIRATION

REFERENCES

The sections below contain references to educational and scientific research to support the claims we made in this book. Throughout the book, we contextualized the research and provided summaries of research studies; therefore, below you'll only find the references we used for our research. If you're interested in learning more on a particular topic or study, you can use the references below to find the sources.

INTRODUCTION

Anderson, Lorin, and David Krathwohl, eds. 2001. *A Taxonomy for Learning, Teaching and Assessing: A Revision of Bloom's Taxonomy of Educational Objectives*. New York: Longman.

Bloom, Benjamin S. 1956. *Taxonomy of Educational Objectives*. New York: David McKay Company, Inc.

Carson, Rachel. 1965. *The Sense of Wonder*. New York: HarperCollins.

Durie, Bruce. 2005. "Senses Special: Doors of Perception." *New Scientist*. newscientist.com/article/mg18524841-600-senses-special-doors-of-perception/.

Gilbert, Elizabeth. 2016. *Big Magic: Creative Living Beyond Fear*. New York: Riverhead Books.

Petersik, Sherry. 2017. "Kids Room Ideas from the Cutest Kids Bookstore Ever." Young House Love (blog). younghouselove.com/bookstore-kids-room-ideas.

Plato. 1921. *Plato in Twelve Volumes*. Translated by Harold N. Fowler. Cambridge, MA: Harvard University Press.

SURPRISE

Bishop, Rudine Sims. 1990. "Mirrors, Windows, and Sliding Glass Doors." In *Collective Perspectives: Choosing and Using Books for the Classroom*, edited by Hughes Moir. Norwood, MA: Christopher-Gordon Publishers.

Brown, Roger, and James Kulik. 1977. "Flashbulb Memories." *Cognition* 5, no. 1: 73–99. doi.org/10.1016/0010 -0277(77)90018-X.

Fenker, Daniela, and Hartmut Schütze. 2008. "Learning by Surprise." *Scientific American*. scientificamerican.com/ article/learning-by-surprise.

Johnson, David R. 1973. "The Element of Surprise: An Effective Classroom Technique." *The Mathematics Teacher* 66, no. 1 (January): 13–16. jstor.org/stable/27959162.

King, Hope, and Wade King. 2018. *The Wild Card: 7 Steps to an Educator's Creative Breakthrough*. San Diego, CA: Dave Burgess Consulting, Inc.

Luna, Tania, and LeeAnn Renninger, PhD. 2015. *Surprise: Embrace the Unpredictable and Engineer the Unexpected*. New York: Penguin.

Marzano, Robert J. 2007. *The Art and Science of Teaching: A Comprehensive Framework for Effective Instruction*. Alexandria, VA: Association for Supervision and Curriculum Development.

Stahl, Aimee E., and Lisa Feigenson. 2015. "Observing the Unexpected Enhances Infants' Learning and Exploration." *Science* 348, no. 6230 (April): 91–94. doi.org/10.1126/ science.aaa3799.

Willis, Judy. 2006. *Research-Based Strategies to Ignite Student Learning: Insights from a Neurologist and Classroom Teacher*. Alexandria, VA: Association for Supervision and Curriculum Development.

CURIOSITY

Burgess, Dave. 2012. *Teach Like a Pirate*. San Diego, CA: Dave Burgess Consulting, Inc.

Engel, Susan. 2011. "Children's Need to Know: Curiosity in Schools." *Harvard Educational Review* 81, no. 4 (December): 625–645. doi.org/10.17763/haer.81.4.h054131316473115.

Engel, Susan. 2015. *The Hungry Mind: The Origins of Curiosity in Childhood*. Cambridge, MA: Harvard Press.

Gordon, Goren, Cynthia Breazeal, and Susan Engel. 2015. "Can Children Catch Curiosity from a Social Robot?" *HRI 2015: Proceedings of the Tenth Annual ACM/IEEE International Conference on Human-Robot Interaction* (March): 91–98. doi.org/10.1145/2696454.2696469.

Gruber, Matthias J., Bernard D. Gelman, and Charan Ranganath. 2014. "States of Curiosity Modulate Hippocampus-Dependent Learning via the Dopaminergic Circuit." *Neuron* 84, no. 2 (October): 486–496. doi.org/10.1016/j.neuron.2014.08.060.

Hilton. 2018. "New Survey Explores Link Between Travel and Curiosity." hospitalitynet.org/news/4089338.html.

Johnson, David W., and Roger T. Johnson. 1988. "Critical Thinking Through Structured Controversy." *Educational Leadership* 45, no. 8 (May): 58–64.

Kang, Min Jeong, Ming Hsu, Ian M. Krajbich, George Loewenstein, Samuel M. McClure, Joseph Tao-yi Wang, and Colin F. Camerer. 2009. "The Wick in the Candle of Learning: Epistemic Curiosity Activates Reward Circuitry and Enhances Memory." *Psychological Science* 20, no. 8 (August): 963–973. doi.org/10.1111/j.1467-9280.2009.02402.x.

Konnikova, Maria. 2011. "Clean Hands, Clean Minds: The Psychological Impact of Physical Cleanliness." Big Think. bigthink.com/artful-choice/clean-hands-clean-minds-the-psychological-impact-of-physical-cleanliness.

Leslie, Ian. 2015. *Curious: The Desire to Know and Why Your Future Depends on It.* New York: Basic Books.

Ostroff, Wendy L. 2016. *Cultivating Curiosity in K-12 Classrooms.* Alexandria, VA: Association for Supervision and Curriculum Development.

Rick Steves' Europe. 2020. ricksteves.com.

Shah, Prachi E., Heidi M. Weeks, Blair Richards, and Niko Kaciroti. 2018. "Early Childhood Curiosity and Kindergarten Reading and Math Academic Achievement." *Pediatric Research* 84: 380–386. doi.org/10.1038/s41390-018-0039-3.

Sousa, David. 2016. *How the Brain Learns.* 5th ed. Toronto, ON: Corwin.

Trussler, Marc, and Stuart Soroka. 2014. "Consumer Demand for Cynical and Negative News Frames." *The International Journal of Press/Politics* 19, no. 3 (March): 360–379. dx.doi .org/10.1177/1940161214524832.

von Stumm, Sophie, Benedikt Hell, and Tomas Chamorro-Premuzic. 2011. "The Hungry Mind: Intellectual Curiosity Is the Third Pillar of Academic Performance." *Perspectives on Psychological Science* 6, no. 6 (October): 574–588. doi.org/10 .1177/1745691611421204.

Weisman Art Museum. 2020. "Perceive." wam.umn.edu/ education/artful-writing/perceive/.

Yuhas, Daisy. 2018. "Piqued: The Case for Curiosity." The Hechinger Report. hechingerreport.org/piqued-the-case -for-curiosity.

FREEDOM

Anderson-McNamee, Jona K., and Sandra J. Bailey. 2010. "The Importance of Play in Early Childhood Development." tulsaeducare.org/wp-content/uploads/2012/01/Educare -Content-G-Articles-Importance-of-Play-Article.pdf.

Andrade, Heidi L., and Gavin T. L. Brown, eds. 2016. "Student Self-Assessment in the Classroom." In *Handbook of Human and Social Conditions in Assessment*, 319–334. London: Routledge.

Cain, Susan. 2013. *Quiet: The Power of Introverts in a World That Can't Stop Talking*. New York: Random House.

Carlson, Jordan A., Jessa K. Engelberg, Kelli L. Cain, Terry L. Conway, Alex M. Mignano, Edith A. Bonilla, Carrie Geremia, and James F. Sallis. 2015. "Implementing Classroom Physical Activity Breaks: Associations with Student Physical Activity and Classroom Behavior." *Preventive Medicine* 81 (December): 67–72. doi.org/10.1016/j.ypmed.2015.08.006.

CAST. 2018. Universal Design for Learning Guidelines version 2.2. udlguidelines.cast.org.

Cook, Susan Wagner, Terina KuangYi Yip, and Susan Goldin-Meadow. 2010. "Gesturing Makes Memories That Last." *Journal of Memory and Language* 63, no. 4 (November): 465–475. doi.org/10.1016/j.jml.2010.07.002.

Donnelly, Joseph E., and Kate Lambourne. 2011. "Classroom-Based Physical Activity, Cognition, and Academic Achievement." *Preventive Medicine* 52, Suppl. 1 (June): S36–S42. doi.org/10.1016/j.ypmed.2011.01.021.

Double, Kit S., Joshua A. McGrane, and Therese N. Hopfenbeck. 2019. "The Impact of Peer Assessment on Academic Performance: A Meta-analysis of Control Group Studies." *Educational Psychology Review* 32 (December): 481–509. doi.org/10.1007/s10648-019-09510-3.

Emerson, Ralph Waldo. 1967. "Self-Reliance." White Plains, NY: Peter Pauper Press.

Fabio, Michelle. 2019. "How the Socratic Method Works and Why Is It Used in Law School." ThoughtCo. thoughtco.com/what-is-the-socratic-method-2154875.

Falchikov, Nancy, and Judy Goldfinch. 2000. "Student Peer Assessment in Higher Education: A Meta-Analysis

Comparing Peer and Teacher Marks." *Review of Educational Research* 70, no. 3 (Fall): 287–322. jstor.org/stable/1170785.

Fisher, Douglas, and Gay Ivey. 2007. "Farewell to *A Farewell to Arms*: Deemphasizing the Whole-Class Novel." *Phi Delta Kappan* 88, no. 7 (March): 494–497. doi.org/10.1177/003172170708800706.

Freire, Paulo. 1972. *Pedagogy of the Oppressed*. New York: Herder and Herder.

Kohn, Alfie. 2016. "Your Hand's Not Raised? Too Bad: I'm Calling on You Anyway." alfiekohn.org/blogs/hands.

Kreber, Carolin, Charles Anderson, Noel Entwhistle, and Jan McArthur. 2014. *Advances and Innovations in University Assessment and Feedback*. Edinburgh University Press. jstor.org/stable/10.3366/j.ctt14brxp5.

Love, Bettina. 2019. *We Want to Do More Than Survive: Abolitionist Teaching and the Pursuit of Educational Freedom.* Boston: Beacon Press.

Mahar, Matthew T., Sheila K. Murphy, David A. Rowe, Jeannie Golden, A. Tamlyn Shields, and Thomas D. Raedeke. 2006. "Effects of a Classroom-Based Program on Physical Activity and On-Task Behavior." *Medicine and Science in Sports and Exercise* 38, no. 12 (December): 2086–2094. doi.org/10.1249/01.mss.0000235359.16685.a3.

McMillan, James H., and Jessica Hearn. 2008. "Student Self-Assessment: The Key to Stronger Student Motivation and Higher Achievement." *Educational Horizons* 87, no. 1 (Fall): 40–49. jstor.org/stable/42923742.

Oppezzo, Marily, and Daniel L. Schwartz. 2014. "Give Your Ideas Some Legs: The Positive Effect of Walking on Creative Thinking." *Journal of Experimental Psychology: Learning, Memory, and Cognition* 40, no. 4: 1142–1152. doi.org/10.1037/a0036577.

Patall, Erika A., Harris Cooper, and Susan R. Wynn. 2010. "The Effectiveness and Relative Importance of Choice in the Classroom." *Journal of Educational Psychology* 102, no. 4: 896–915. doi.org/10.1037/a0019545.

Probst, Robert E. 2004. *Response & Analysis: Teaching Literature in Secondary School*. 2nd ed. Portsmouth, NH: Heinemann.

Ratey, John, and Eric Hagerman. 2011. *Spark: The Revolutionary New Science of Exercise and the Brain*. New York: Little, Brown Spark.

Rogers, Carl. 1969. *Freedom to Learn*. Columbus, OH: Charles E. Merrill Publishing Company.

Stone, Nic. 2018. "2018 Proved Black Kids Read (and White Kids Read Books with Black Leads)." *HuffPost.* huffpost.com/entry/opinion-ya-books-black-leads_n_5c2136a4e4b05c88b6fb6a4b.

Strickland, Kathleen, and James Strickland. 2002. *Engaged in Learning*. Portsmouth, NH: Heinemann.

van den Berg, Ineke, Wilfried Admiraal, and Albert Pilot. 2006. "Designing Student Peer Assessment in Higher Education: Analysis of Written and Oral Peer Feedback." *Teaching in Higher Education* 11, no. 2 (August): 135–147. doi.org/10.1080/13562510500527685.

Wong, Harry K., and Rosemary T. Wong. 2009. *The First Days of School: How to Be an Effective Teacher*. Mountain View, CA: Harry K. Wong Publications.

INSPIRATION

Berman, Marc G., John Jonides, and Stephen Kaplan. 2008. "The Cognitive Benefits of Interacting with Nature." *Psychological Science* 19, no. 12 (December): 1207–1212. doi.org/10.1111/j.1467-9280.2008.02225.x.

Bryant, Debra. 2017. "Embrace Art in the Classroom Discover Art Is Not Scary Become Capable and Confident." *Educating Young Children: Learning and Teaching in the Early Childhood*

Years 23, no. 1 (Spring): 13–16. search.informit.org/doi/10.
3316/INFORMIT.835687204690205.

Burkley, Melissa. 2017. "'Get Some Fresh Air' to Boost Your
Creativity." *Psychology Today.* psychologytoday.com/za/
blog/the-social-thinker/201712/get-some-fresh-air-boost
-your-creativity.

Carey, Benedict. 2010. "Forget What You Know About Good Study
Habits." *The New York Times.* nytimes.com/2010/09/07/
health/views/07mind.html.

Cho, Hyunju, Seokjin Ryu, Jeeae Noh, and Jongsun Lee. 2016.
"The Effectiveness of Daily Mindful Breathing Practices on
Test Anxiety of Students." *PLOS One* 11, no. 10 (October):
e0164822. doi.org/10.1371/journal.pone.0164822.

Conaway, Cameron. 2019. "As the Workforce Transforms,
Creativity Must Take Priority." *Forbes.* forbes.com/sites/
forbescommunicationscouncil/2019/09/04/as-the
-workforce-transforms-creativity-must-take-priority/
#4b2fcd4564f6.

Copper, Jenna. 2020. "Using ICT to Establish and Facilitate Global
Connections in K-12 Education." In *The Roles of Technology
and Globalization in Educational Transformation*, edited by
Blessing F. Adeoye and Gladys Arome, 206–220. IGI Global.
doi.org/10.4018/978-1-5225-9746-9.ch016.

Csikszentmihalyi, Mihaly. 2013. *Creativity: Flow and the Psychology
of Discovery and Invention*. New York: Harper Perennial.

Dewey, John. 1991. "The Sources of a Science of Education."
In *The Later Works of John Dewey, 1925–1953: Volume 16,
1949–1952*, edited by Jo Ann Boydston, 1–40. Carbondale,
IL: Southern Illinois University Press.

Dionne, Michelle, Silvia Diazgranados Ferrans, Tracy Elizabeth,
and Robert L. Selman. 2014. *An Educator's Guide to
Promoting Perspective Taking Skills in the Classroom: The
Survey of Students' Perspective Taking Skills*. Strategic

Education Research Project, Institute for the Catalyzing Comprehension through Discussion and Debate Project.

Doron, Eyal. 2017. "Fostering Creativity in School Aged Children Through Perspective Taking and Visual Media Based Short Term Intervention Program." *Thinking Skills and Creativity* 23 (March): 150–160. doi.org/10.1016/j.tsc.2016.12.003.

Fetell Lee, Ingrid. 2018. *Joyful: The Surprising Power of Ordinary Things to Create Extraordinary Happiness*. New York: Little, Brown Spark.

Fink, Andreas, Roland H. Grabner, Daniela Gebauer, Gernot Reishofer, Karl Koschutnig, and Franz Ebner. 2010. "Enhancing Creativity by Means of Cognitive Stimulation: Evidence from an fMRI Study." *NeuroImage* 52, no. 4 (October): 1687–1695. doi.org/10.1016/j.neuroimage .2010.05.072.

Flook, Lisa, Susan L. Smalley, M. Jennifer Kitil, Brian M. Galla, Susan Kaiser-Greenland, Jill Locke, Eric Ishijima, and Connie Kasari. 2010. "Effects of Mindful Awareness Practices on Executive Functions in Elementary School Children." *Journal of Applied School Psychology* 26, no. 1 (February): 70–95. doi.org/10.1080/15377900903379125.

Galinksy, Ellen. 2010. *Mind in the Making: The Seven Essential Life Skills Every Child Needs*. New York: Harper Collins.

Jia, Lile, Edward R. Hirt, and Samuel C. Karpen. 2009. "Lessons from a Faraway Land: The Effect of Spatial Distance on Creative Cognition." *Journal of Experimental Social Psychology* 45, no. 5 (September): 1127–1131. doi.org/10.1016/j.jesp .2009.05.015.

Joubert, Mathilda Marie. 2001. "The Art of Creative Teaching: NACCCE and Beyond." In *Creativity in Education*, edited by Anna Craft, Bob Jeffrey, and Mike Leibling, 17–34. London: Continuum.

Land, George. 2011. "The Failure of Success." Filmed at TEDxTucson in Tucson, AZ. Video, 13:06. youtube.com/watch?time_continue=17&v=ZfKMq-rYtnc&feature=emb _title.

Leung, Angela Ka-Yee, William W. Maddux, Adam D. Galinsky, and Chi-yue Chiu. 2008. "Multicultural Experience Enhances Creativity: The When and How." *American Psychologist* 63, no. 3 (April): 169–181. doi.org/10.1037/0003-066X.63.3.169.

Love, Bettina. 2019. *We Want to Do More Than Survive: Abolitionist Teaching and The Pursuit of Educational Freedom.* Boston: Beacon Press.

McNamee, David. 2009. "Hey, What's That Sound: Oblique Strategies." *The Guardian.* theguardian.com/music/2009/sep/07/oblique-strategies.

Metz, Staci M., Jennifer L. Frank, Diane Reibel, Todd Cantrell, Richard Sanders, and Patricia C. Broderick. 2013. "The Effectiveness of the Learning to BREATHE Program on Adolescent Emotion Regulation." *Research in Human Development* 10, no. 3 (August): 252–272. doi.org/10.1080/15427609.2013.818488.

Meyers-Levy, Joan, and Rui Zhu. 2007. "The Influence of Ceiling Height: The Effect of Priming on the Type of Processing That People Use." *Journal of Consumer Research* 34, no. 2 (August): 174–186. doi.org/10.1086/519146.

Morse, Karen. 2017. "Developing Creative Thinking Skills Through Art." *The High Flyer.* National Association for Gifted Children. nagc.org/blog/developing-creative-thinking-skills-through-art-0.

National Advisory Committee on Creative and Cultural Education. 1999. "All Our Futures: Creativity, Culture and Education." sirkenrobinson.com/pdf/allourfutures.pdf.

Nhat Hanh, Thich, and Katherine Weare. 2017. *Happy Teachers Change the World: A Guide for Cultivating Mindfulness in Education.* Berkeley, CA: Parallax Press.

Sharma, Mala. 2019. "Why Creativity Is the Superpower for Tomorrow's Workforce." Adobe (blog). theblog.adobe.com/ why-creativity-is-the-superpower-for-tomorrows-workforce.

Simpson, Douglas, Michael John Brierley Jackson, and Judy C. Aycock. 2005. *John Dewey and the Art of Teaching: Toward Reflective and Imaginative Practic*e. Thousand Oaks, CA: Sage Publications.

Stone, Matthew J., and James F. Petrick. 2013. "The Educational Benefits of Travel Experiences: A Literature Review." *Journal of Travel Research* 52, no. 6 (August): 731–744. doi.org/10 .1177/0047287513500588.

Sun, Jiangzhou, et al. 2016. "Training Your Brain to Be More Creative: Brain Functional and Structural Changes Induced by Divergent Thinking Training." *Human Brain Mapping* 37, no. 10 (October): 3375–3387.

Suttie, Jill. 2016. "How Nature Can Make You Kinder, Happier, and More Creative." *Greater Good Magazine*. The Greater Good Science Center at UC Berkeley. greatergood.berkeley.edu/ article/item/how_nature_makes_you_kinder_happier _more_creative.

Swart, Tara. 2019. *The Source: The Secrets of the Universe, the Science of the Brain*. New York: HarperOne.

Walker, Rob. 2019. *The Art of Noticing: 131 Ways to Spark Creativity, Find Inspiration, and Discover Joy in the Everyday*. New York: Alfred A. Knopf.

World Economic Forum. 2018. "The Future of Jobs Report 2018." Geneva: World Economic Forum.

Yenawine, Philip. 2013. *Visual Thinking Strategies: Using Art to Deepen Learning Across School Disciplines.* Cambridge, MA: Harvard Education Press.

Yoga Ed. 2017. yogaed.com.

ACKNOWLEDGMENTS

To our KTW Wonder Makers (our guest presenters and writers, workshop attendees, virtual workshop members, readers, and friends):

YOU have made Keeping the Wonder a magical mission. Thank you for believing in the wonder of learning. Thank you for following us to enchanting book shops, charming castles, and now, the pages of this book. We feel incredibly lucky that we are able to do what we love, in our classrooms and across the country.

When your teaching energy is in one room, it is pure magic. Your energy and enthusiasm motivate us to keep the wonder, joy, and magic in learning. Without fellow teachers like you, we would not have had the chance to share our mission and write this book. Thank you from the bottom of our hearts!

To Ashley: You are OUR Wonder Maker! From your magical mood boards to your marvelous decor to your wondrous way of working through every challenge, you always manage to surprise us with your creativity. We are so thankful for your hard work, dedication, and friendship. Thank you for bringing us along on this magical ride!

To Jenna: Thank you for daring to dream. Moments after our very first workshop, you declared that we had a book in us. In your confident and dedicated way, you persisted until you made our dream a reality, and for that we are grateful. This book is here because of you.

With that said, **Dave, Shelley, and DBC publishing team**, thank you for giving us a chance to put our wonder to the page! You have been a joy to work with, and we are proud to be part of a team that strives to keep the wonder in education.

*Jenna

To my husband, Mike: Thank you for making me laugh, reading my writing, patting me on the back, and of course, making me amazing dinners. From the moment I saw you, I knew you were the one. I am so lucky that I get to live this life with you. I love you more than words!

To my mom: Thank you for reading and copyediting this book (and everything else I've ever written)! I can't ever thank you enough for all you do for me. You are my best friend, and you mean the world to me. I love you, Mom!

To my dad: Thank you for being my personal mechanic, counselor, coach, contractor, landscaper, car salesman, and everything in between. Thank you for always coming to the rescue when something breaks or goes wrong and, of course, for being the #1 dad! I love you!

To my "little" brothers, Mikey and John: Thank you for always having my back. How lucky I am to have two people in this world whom I know I can always count on. Your big sis is so proud of you!

To Dr. Semich, Dr. Permenter, and Dr. Strickland: Thank you for encouraging me, supporting me, and teaching me. You have made such a wonderful impact on my life.

To my former teachers, coaches, professors, and mentors: Thank you. I am so thankful to have had such kind, dedicated, and talented teachers, coaches, professors, and mentors from Neshannock to Slippery Rock to Robert Morris.

To my second-grade teacher, Mrs. Bakuhn: Thank you for showing me my first and most wonderful glimpse at a magical classroom. I hope I can honor you by always keeping the wonder in mine.

To my students: Thank you for inspiring me to keep the wonder in our classroom. May you always remember to tune in to your sense of wonder. I believe in you!

To my daughters, Gianna and Camilla: You bring so much magic into our world. You surprise us with your ingenuity every single day. You show us that curiosity will bring us on adventures we could never have imagined. You remind us to seek out freedom to explore, play, and dream. You are my inspiration. I love you to the moon and back.

To my mother: Thank you for reading to me every night as a child; I suspect it made all the difference.

To my stepfather: Thank you for your support and behind-the-scenes help that gave me the time to make my dreams come true.

To my grandparents: Thank you for always encouraging my imaginative play and for declaring all of my creations the "BEST THING EVER." I hope that you think the same of this book.

To my father: Thank you for sparking my wanderlust. You were always the adventurous soul I hoped to be, and without that trait, none of this would have been.

To my husband, Aaron: You believe in my wild ideas not only with your words but with your actions. From helping me set up workshops to cooking dinner every night while I write, none of this would be possible without your endless love and support. You, my dear, make life wonderful.

To my best friends: Thank you for traveling with me to my first workshop. Though you aren't teachers, you enthusiastically cheered me on and have since encouraged me every step of the way. Also, our after-parties are my favorite.

To my former teachers: You made such an impact on my life that I aspired to be one of you, and I believe that is the ultimate compliment. Thank you for everything, truly.

To my students: I hope that I have taught and inspired you half as much as you have me. May you become lifelong learners and wonderers!

To my mom and dad: Thank you for your endless support and unconditional love. Thank you for surrounding me with piles of books, blank pages, and the opportunities that led me to where I am today. I love you and appreciate you more than you know.

To my siblings, Jessie, Molly, Andy, and Maddie: Thank you for always being there for me, even when I forced you to "play school" and be my students when we were growing up. I can't imagine a life without the love and laughter we share.

To Tony: Thank you for your love, support, and constant encouragement, especially when I didn't think I had it in me to present at a workshop or write this book. You are always able to remind me of my passion for teaching and my purpose in life. For that, I am thankful.

To all of my former teachers, especially Jayme Bales and Dr. Mary McGann: Thank you to all of my former teachers who molded me into who I am today. I am so thankful that I was blessed with incredible teachers who inspired me to become an educator, too. A special thanks to my fourth-grade teacher, Jayme Bales, who once sent me home with a little blank book and told me I would be a writer one day. You made all the difference. Thank you, too, to Dr. Mary McGann, for the reminder that my students should always be working harder than me. That philosophy sparked my shift to a more creative, curious, and student-centered classroom.

To all of my past and present colleagues and teacher friends, especially Malerie: Thank you for your support, guidance, and encouragement. Malerie, thank you for always being there for me, whether we are across the hall, on a workshop road trip, or a phone call away.

To my former, current, and future students: Being your teacher is the greatest gift. You are, and always will be, my joy, my wonder, and my reason.

Staci

To my mom: Even thirty years later, you still remind me every day of how proud you are of me. I love you.

To my great-aunt Eileen: I hope I'm as cool as you when I'm 96. I don't even know how to sum up all that you have done for me. Thank you for absolutely everything.

To my longest friend, Justin: Thank you for telling me, "I think you should become a teacher." That one decision changed the entire trajectory of my life.

To my colleague turned best friend and roommate, Anna: I will forever be grateful for you joining me on all of the Keeping the Wonder adventures and for all the joy and wonder you have brought to my life, even if you do sing, a lot, on our road trips.

To my tenth-grade Honors English teacher, Barbara Foxx: The work ethic you instilled in me and the love of English speak volumes about your work as an educator. I aspire to be like you always.

To my students: You are the wonder and magic of education, and you change my life for the better every single day.

ABOUT THE AUTHORS

JENNA COPPER

Jenna Copper is a high school English teacher in Pennsylvania and an instructional specialist who designs curriculum and presents professional development for educators. Earning her PhD in Instruction and Leadership, she is passionate about conducting and sharing educational research and has presented her work at national and state conferences such as NCTE, PCTELA, and SITE. As an author

Photo by Kelsey Converse Photography

and co-author, her work has appeared in journals, textbooks, and online publications with AACE, IGI Global, Read Write Think, and We Are Teachers. She is a lead presenter for the Keeping the Wonder Workshop, specializing in lenses of learning and engaging reading and writing instruction. You can find out more about her research and resources at her website, jennacopper.com, and on Instagram at @drjennacopper.

ASHLEY BIBLE

In addition to being a high school English teacher in East Tennessee, Ashley Bible is a workshop creator and resource designer. As a first-generation college graduate, she proudly earned her Master of Arts in English Literature, which has served her well as a teacher, author, and lifelong learner. You can read more about her work on her blog at buildingbooklove.com and on Instagram at @buildingbooklove.

Photo by Kelsey Converse Photography

ABBY GROSS

Although she recently fell in love with teaching middle school reading, Abby Gross has spent most of her career teaching high school English, including American Literature, Journalism, Newspaper, Technical Communication, and more. Abby is committed to crafting student-centered learning experiences that engage and empower her students. When she's not teaching, you can find

Photo by Kelsey Converse Photography

Abby designing resources, blogging, and helping other teachers. In addition to facilitating student engagement workshop sessions at Keeping the Wonder, she has led professional development on integrating technology and presented on multi-genre text sets at NCTE. You can check out Abby's ideas and tech tips on her blog at writeonwithmissg.com, on Instagram at @writeonwithmissg, and on Twitter at @writeonwmissg.

STACI LAMB

Staci Lamb is an English teacher in Maryland and served as the 2018 Cecil County Teacher of the Year and 2018 finalist for the state. Staci was also the recipient of the 2019 Maryland NEA Foundations in Teaching Excellence Award. She has a bachelor's degree in English Education from University of Delaware and is pursuing her master's degree in Transformational Educational Leadership at Towson

Photo by Kelsey Converse Photography

University. In the summer, she teaches for University of Delaware's Upward Bound Math and Science program. You can find tips and resources on Staci's blog at theengagingstation.com or on Instagram at @theengagingstation.

ABOUT KEEPING THE WONDER

Keeping the Wonder Workshop was established in 2017 by Ashley Bible when she was inspired to bring together English teachers at a magical bookstore in Monroe, Georgia. Since then, it's been our mission to create hands-on workshop-style professional development events at magical venues across the US. Our workshops will leave you feeling inspired to engage your students in reading and prepared to help them master their standards. Hosted by the core four and supported by amazing guest presenters, Keeping the Wonder is perfect for high school, middle school, and upper elementary teachers who want to learn teacher-tested strategies that will help them connect their students to the magic of learning.

To find out the location of our next workshop, become a member of a virtual Keeping the Wonder Workshop, or book speaking engagements, go to

keepingthewonderworkshop.com

and join us at @keepingthewonder on Instagram.

MORE FROM
Dave Burgess Consulting, Inc.

Since 2012, DBCI has been publishing books that inspire and equip educators to be their best. For more information on our titles or to purchase bulk orders for your school, district, or book study, visit **DaveBurgessconsulting.com/DBCIbooks**.

MORE INSPIRATION, PROFESSIONAL GROWTH & PERSONAL DEVELOPMENT

Be REAL by Tara Martin
Be the One for Kids by Ryan Sheehy
The Coach ADVenture by Amy Illingworth
Creatively Productive by Lisa Johnson
Educational Eye Exam by Alicia Ray
The EduNinja Mindset by Jennifer Burdis
Empower Our Girls by Lynmara Colón and Adam Welcome
Finding Lifelines by Andrew Grieve and Andrew Sharos
The Four O'Clock Faculty by Rich Czyz
How Much Water Do We Have? by Pete and Kris Nunweiler
P Is for Pirate by Dave and Shelley Burgess
A Passion for Kindness by Tamara Letter
The Path to Serendipity by Allyson Apsey
Sanctuaries by Dan Tricarico
Saving Sycamore by Molly B. Hudgens

The SECRET SAUCE by Rich Czyz

Shattering the Perfect Teacher Myth by Aaron Hogan

Stories from Webb by Todd Nesloney

Talk to Me by Kim Bearden

Teach Better by Chad Ostrowski, Tiffany Ott, Rae Hughart, and Jeff Gargas

Teach Me, Teacher by Jacob Chastain

Teach, Play, Learn! by Adam Peterson

The Teachers of Oz by Herbie Raad and Nathan Lang-Raad

TeamMakers by Laura Robb and Evan Robb

Through the Lens of Serendipity by Allyson Apsey

The Zen Teacher by Dan Tricarico

LIKE A PIRATE™ SERIES

Teach Like a PIRATE by Dave Burgess

eXPlore Like a PIRATE by Michael Matera

Learn Like a PIRATE by Paul Solarz

Play Like a PIRATE by Quinn Rollins

Run Like a PIRATE by Adam Welcome

Tech Like a PIRATE by Matt Miller

LEAD LIKE A PIRATE™ SERIES

Lead Like a PIRATE by Shelley Burgess and Beth Houf

Balance Like a PIRATE by Jessica Cabeen, Jessica Johnson, and Sarah Johnson

Lead beyond Your Title by Nili Bartley

Lead with Appreciation by Amber Teamann and Melinda Miller

Lead with Culture by Jay Billy

Lead with Instructional Rounds by Vicki Wilson

Lead with Literacy by Mandy Ellis

LEADERSHIP & SCHOOL CULTURE

Beyond the Surface of Restorative Practices by Marisol Rerucha

Choosing to See by Pamela Seda and Kyndall Brown

Culturize by Jimmy Casas

Escaping the School Leader's Dunk Tank by Rebecca Coda and
    Rick Jetter

Fight Song by Kim Bearden

From Teacher to Leader by Starr Sackstein

If the Dance Floor Is Empty, Change the Song by Joe Clark

The Innovator's Mindset by George Couros

It's OK to Say "They" by Christy Whittlesey

Kids Deserve It! by Todd Nesloney and Adam Welcome

Let Them Speak by Rebecca Coda and Rick Jetter

The Limitless School by Abe Hege and Adam Dovico

Live Your Excellence by Jimmy Casas

Next-Level Teaching by Jonathan Alsheimer

The Pepper Effect by Sean Gaillard

Principaled by Kate Barker, Kourtney Ferrua, and Rachael George

The Principled Principal by Jeffrey Zoul and Anthony McConnell

Relentless by Hamish Brewer

The Secret Solution by Todd Whitaker, Sam Miller, and Ryan Donlan

Start. Right. Now. by Todd Whitaker, Jeffrey Zoul, and Jimmy Casas

Stop. Right. Now. by Jimmy Casas and Jeffrey Zoul

Teachers Deserve It by Rae Hughart and Adam Welcome

Teach Your Class Off by CJ Reynolds

They Call Me "Mr. De" by Frank DeAngelis

Thrive through the Five by Jill M. Siler

Unmapped Potential by Julie Hasson and Missy Lennard

When Kids Lead by Todd Nesloney and Adam Dovico

Word Shift by Joy Kirr

Your School Rocks by Ryan McLane and Eric Lowe

TECHNOLOGY & TOOLS

50 Things to Go Further with Google Classroom by Alice Keeler and
    Libbi Miller

50 Things You Can Do with Google Classroom by Alice Keeler and
    Libbi Miller

140 Twitter Tips for Educators by Brad Currie, Billy Krakower, and
  Scott Rocco
Block Breaker by Brian Aspinall
Building Blocks for Tiny Techies by Jamila "Mia" Leonard
Code Breaker by Brian Aspinall
The Complete EdTech Coach by Katherine Goyette and Adam Juarez
Control Alt Achieve by Eric Curts
The Esports Education Playbook by Chris Aviles, Steve Isaacs,
  Christine Lion-Bailey, and Jesse Lubinsky
Google Apps for Littles by Christine Pinto and Alice Keeler
Master the Media by Julie Smith
Reality Bytes by Christine Lion-Bailey, Jesse Lubinsky, and
  Micah Shippee, PhD
Sail the 7 Cs with Microsoft Education by Becky Keene and
  Kathi Kersznowski
Shake Up Learning by Kasey Bell
Social LEADia by Jennifer Casa-Todd
Stepping Up to Google Classroom by Alice Keeler and Kimberly Mattina
Teaching Math with Google Apps by Alice Keeler and Diana Herrington
Teachingland by Amanda Fox and Mary Ellen Weeks

TEACHING METHODS & MATERIALS

All 4s and 5s by Andrew Sharos
Boredom Busters by Katie Powell
The Classroom Chef by John Stevens and Matt Vaudrey
The Collaborative Classroom by Trevor Muir
Copyrighteous by Diana Gill
CREATE by Bethany J. Petty
Ditch That Homework by Matt Miller and Alice Keeler
Ditch That Textbook by Matt Miller
Don't Ditch That Tech by Matt Miller, Nate Ridgway, and
  Angelia Ridgway
EDrenaline Rush by John Meehan
Educated by Design by Michael Cohen, The Tech Rabbi

The EduProtocol Field Guide by Marlena Hebern and Jon Corippo

The EduProtocol Field Guide: Book 2 by Marlena Hebern and Jon Corippo

The EduProtocol Field Guide: Math Edition by Lisa Nowakowski and Jeremiah Ruesch

Game On? Brain On! by Lindsay Portnoy, PhD

Guided Math AMPED by Reagan Tunstall

Innovating Play by Jessica LaBar-Twomy and Christine Pinto

Instant Relevance by Denis Sheeran

LAUNCH by John Spencer and A.J. Juliani

Make Learning MAGICAL by Tisha Richmond

Pass the Baton by Kathryn Finch and Theresa Hoover

Project-Based Learning Anywhere by Lori Elliott

Pure Genius by Don Wettrick

The Revolution by Darren Ellwein and Derek McCoy

Shift This! by Joy Kirr

Skyrocket Your Teacher Coaching by Michael Cary Sonbert

Spark Learning by Ramsey Musallam

Sparks in the Dark by Travis Crowder and Todd Nesloney

Table Talk Math by John Stevens

Unpack Your Impact by Naomi O'Brien and LaNesha Tabb

The Wild Card by Hope and Wade King

The Writing on the Classroom Wall by Steve Wyborney

You Are Poetry by Mike Johnston

CHILDREN'S BOOKS

Beyond Us by Aaron Polansky

Cannonball In by Tara Martin

Dolphins in Trees by Aaron Polansky

I Want to Be a Lot by Ashley Savage

The Princes of Serendip by Allyson Apsey

Ride with Emilio by Richard Nares

The Wild Card Kids by Hope and Wade King

Zom-Be a Design Thinker by Amanda Fox

Made in the USA
Las Vegas, NV
04 September 2021

29579463R00148